ELECTRIC GUITAR BOOK 1

by Jeff Schroedl

DIGITAL DOWNLOAD CODE
To access audio visit:
www.halleonard.com/mylibrary/gc

Enter Code
8660-2378-8844-7088

ISBN 978-1-4950-7649-7

Published in cooperation between GC LESSONS and

7777 W. BLUEMOUND RD. P.O. BOX 13819 MILWAUKEE, WI 53213

Visit Hal Leonard Online at
www.halleonard.com

Visit Guitar Center Lessons Online at
www.guitarcenter.com/Services/Lessons

MUSIC BASICS

NOTES ON THE STAFF

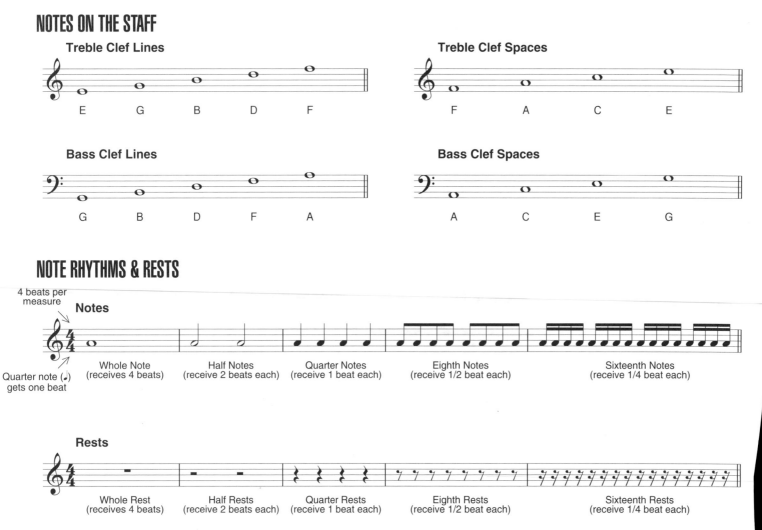

Treble Clef Lines
E G B D F

Treble Clef Spaces
F A C E

Bass Clef Lines
G B D F A

Bass Clef Spaces
A C E G

NOTE RHYTHMS & RESTS

4 beats per measure

Quarter note (♩) gets one beat

Notes

| Whole Note (receives 4 beats) | Half Notes (receive 2 beats each) | Quarter Notes (receive 1 beat each) | Eighth Notes (receive 1/2 beat each) | Sixteenth Notes (receive 1/4 beat each) |

Rests

| Whole Rest (receives 4 beats) | Half Rests (receive 2 beats each) | Quarter Rests (receive 1 beat each) | Eighth Rests (receive 1/2 beat each) | Sixteenth Rests (receive 1/4 beat each) |

MAJOR SCALES

Key	1 (tonic)	2	3	4	5	6	7	8
C major	C	D	E	F	G	A	B	C
G major	G	A	B	C	D	E	F#	G
D major	D	E	F#	G	A	B	C#	D
A major	A	B	C#	D	E	F#	G#	A
E major	E	F#	G#	A	B	C#	D#	E
B major	B	C#	D#	E	F#	G#	A#	B
F# major	F#	G#	A#	B	C#	D#	E#	F#
Db major	Db	Eb	F	Gb	Ab	Bb	C	Db
Ab major	Ab	Bb	C	Db	Eb	F	G	Ab
Eb major	Eb	F	G	Ab	Bb	C	D	Eb
Bb major	Bb	C	D	Eb	F	G	A	Bb
F major	F	G	A	Bb	C	D	E	F

CHAPTER 1
GETTING STARTED

PARTS OF THE GUITAR

This method is designed for use with an electric or acoustic guitar. Both are tuned the same, contain the same notes, and have mostly the same parts. The main difference is that acoustic guitars have a soundhole and are loud enough to be played without amplification, while electric guitars are plugged into an amp.

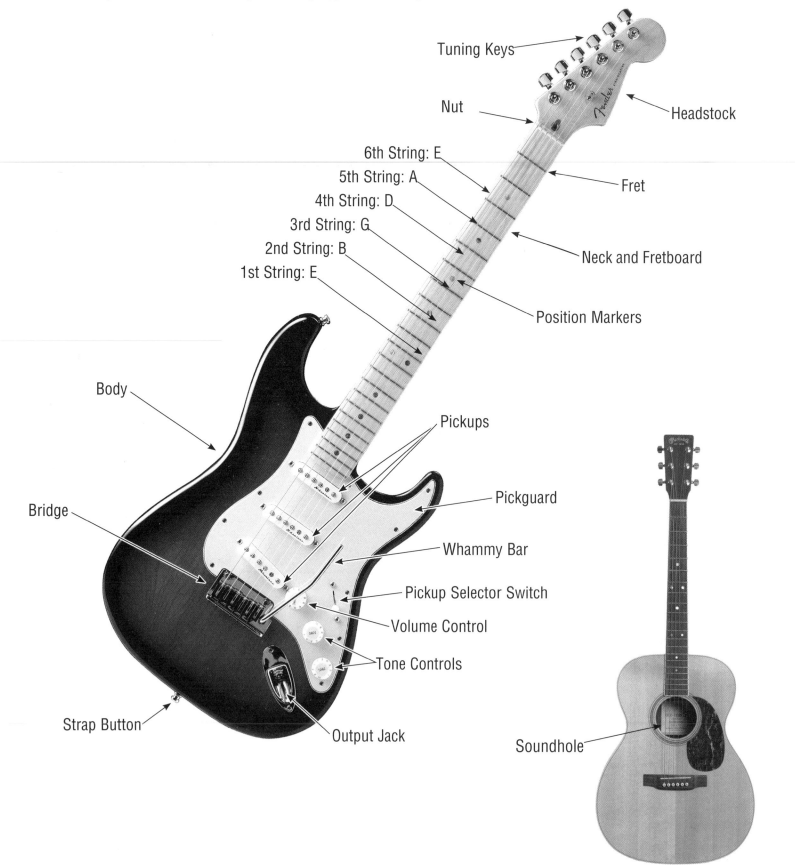

Tuning Keys

Nut

Headstock

6th String: E

5th String: A

Fret

4th String: D

3rd String: G

2nd String: B

Neck and Fretboard

1st String: E

Position Markers

Body

Pickups

Pickguard

Bridge

Whammy Bar

Pickup Selector Switch

Volume Control

Tone Controls

Strap Button

Output Jack

Soundhole

TUNING

The quickest and most accurate way to get in tune is to use an electronic tuner. You can either plug your guitar into the tuner or use the tuner's built-in microphone to tune an acoustic.

The guitar's six open strings should be tuned to these pitches:

E (thickest)–A–D–G–B–E (thinnest)

If you twist a string's tuning key clockwise, the pitch will become lower; if you twist the tuning key counterclockwise, the pitch will become higher.

Adjust the tuning keys until the electronic tuner's meter indicates that the pitch is correct. Or, listen to each string's correct pitch on a piano or keyboard and slowly turn the tuning key until the sound of the string matches the sound on the keyboard.

HOLDING THE GUITAR

Use the pictures below to help find a comfortable playing position. Whether you decide to sit or stand, it's important to remain relaxed and tension-free.

LEFT-HAND POSITION

Fingers are numbered 1 through 4. Arch your fingers and press the strings down firmly between the frets with your fingertips only.

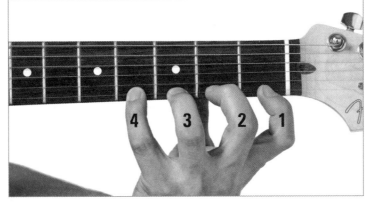

Place your thumb on the underside of the guitar neck. Avoid letting the palm of your hand touch the neck of the guitar.

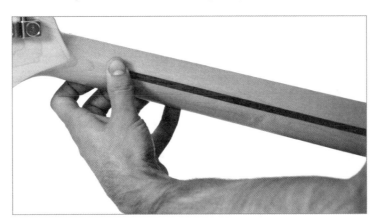

RIGHT-HAND POSITION

Hold the pick between your thumb and index finger. Strike the string with a downward motion approximately halfway between the bridge and neck.

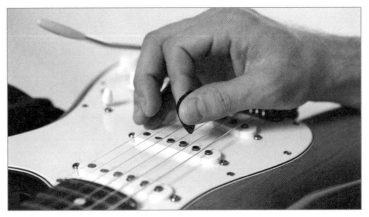

The fingers not holding the pick may rest on the guitar for extra support.

THE LOW E STRING

Guitar music is written in a form of notation called **tablature**, or **tab** for short. Each line represents a string, and each number represents a fret. The thickest string played open, or not pressed, is the low E note. In tab, an open string is represented with a zero (0). The note F is located on the 1st fret. Press, or "fret" the string with your 1st finger, directly behind the first metal fret.

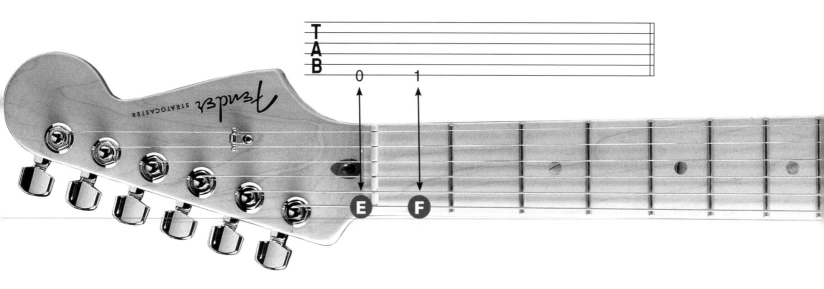

Guitar music can also be written with traditional **notes** on a **staff** in the **treble clef**. From bottom to top, the lines represent the notes E-G-B-D-F and the spaces are F-A-C-E. The low E and F notes on the guitar are written on ledger lines below the staff, like this:

Play the theme from the movie *Jaws* using the notes E and F. Attack the string with a downstroke of the pick. Speed up as the numbers get closer together.

🔊 THEME FROM "'JAWS'

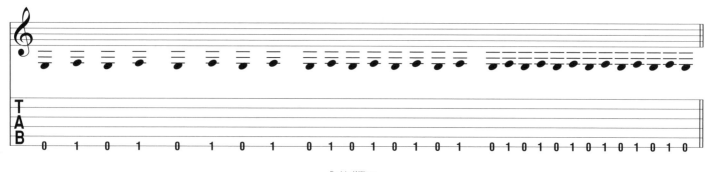

By John Williams
Copyright © 1975 USI B MUSIC PUBLISHING Copyright Renewed All Rights Controlled and Administered by SONGS OF UNIVERSAL, INC.

Now let's learn more notes on the low E string.

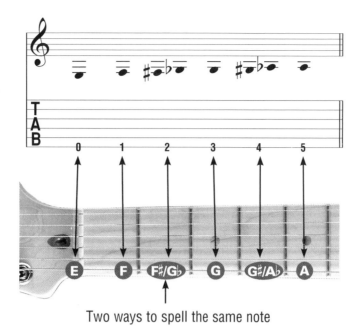

Two ways to spell the same note

GREEN ONIONS

"Green Onions" by Booker T. & the MG's uses the notes E, G, and A. Follow the tab and pick the notes at a steady speed, or **tempo**.

PETER GUNN

A **riff** is a short, composed phrase that is repeated. The popular riff from "Peter Gunn" is played with notes on the low E string.

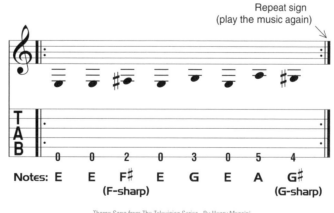

THE A STRING

Here are the notes within the first five frets of the 5th string, called the A string.

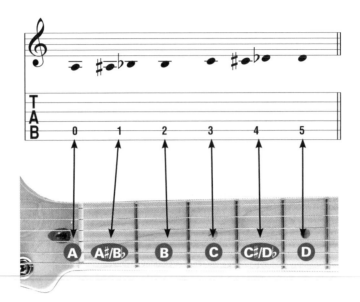

🔊 BRIT ROCK

This catchy riff uses the notes A, B, and C.

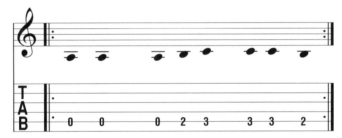

Copyright © 2012 by HAL LEONARD CORPORATION

LEAN ON ME

This song was a #1 hit in two decades. It uses the notes A, B, C#, and D.

Words and Music by Bill Withers
Copyright © 1972 INTERIOR MUSIC CORP.
Copyright Renewed
All Rights Controlled and Administered by SONGS OF UNIVERSAL, INC.

RHYTHM TAB

Rhythm tab adds rhythmic values to the basic tab staff. **Bar lines** divide music into **measures**. A **time signature** tells how many beats are in each measure and what kind of note is counted as one beat. In **4/4 time** ("four-four"), there are four beats in each measure, and a **quarter note** is counted as one beat. It has a vertical stem joined to the tab number.

FEEL THE BEAT

Count "1, 2, 3, 4" as you play.

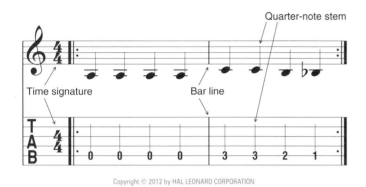

WORKING MAN

This classic riff by the band Rush uses quarter notes on strings 5 and 6.

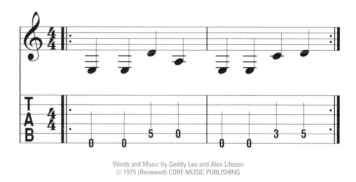

Words and Music by Geddy Lee and Alex Lifeson
© 1975 (Renewed) CORE MUSIC PUBLISHING

ZEPPELIN TRIBUTE

Anchor the palm of your pick hand on the bridge of the guitar to help your picking accuracy.

BLUES RIFF

Use the 3rd finger of your fret hand for notes on the 4th fret, 1st finger for the note on the 2nd fret, and 4th finger (pinky) for the note on the 5th fret.

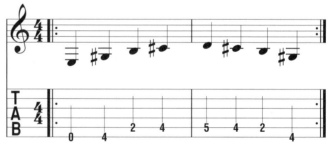

MORE RIFFS

The next two riffs are written in **3/4 time**. This means there are three beats in each measure, and a quarter note receives one beat.

MY NAME IS JONAS

Count "1–2–3, 1–2–3" as you play this riff by the band Weezer.

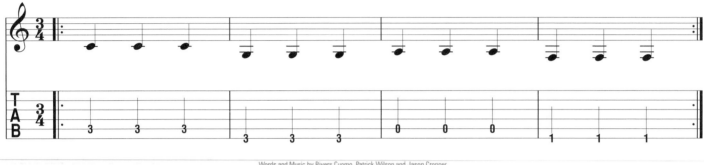

🔊 MALAGUEÑA

This traditional Spanish piece is very popular among classical guitarists.

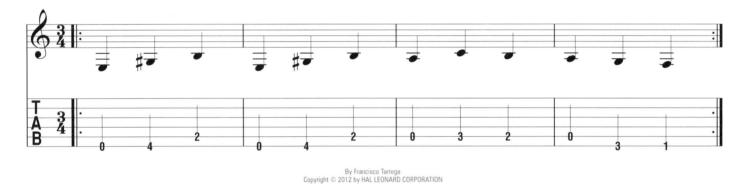

A **half note** lasts two beats. It fills the time of two quarter notes. In tab, a circle surrounds the tab number(s) and is attached to a vertical stem.

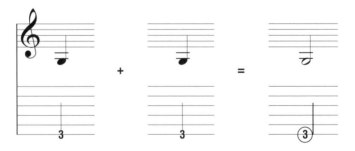

CANON IN D

The first line is played with half notes and the second line is played with quarter notes. Count aloud and keep a steady tempo.

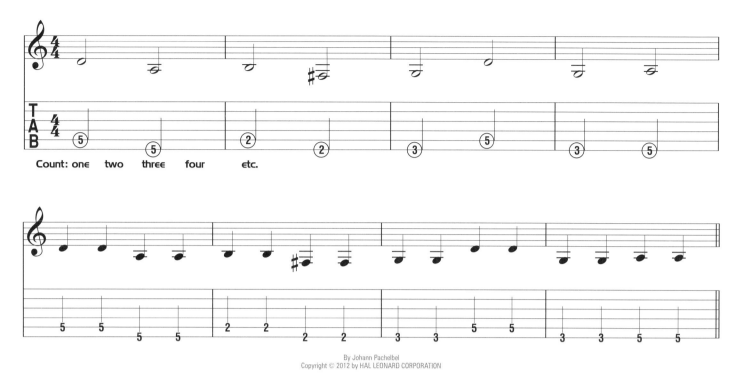

By Johann Pachelbel
Copyright © 2012 by HAL LEONARD CORPORATION

ELECTRIC FUNERAL

The heavy metal band Black Sabbath used half notes and quarter notes for this powerful, eerie riff.

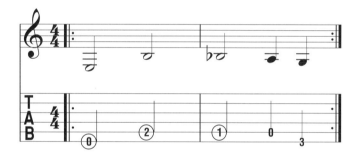

Words and Music by Frank Iommi, John Osbourne, William Ward and Terence Butler
© Copyright 1970 (Renewed) and 1974 (Renewed) Onward Music Ltd., London, England
TRO - Essex Music International, Inc., New York, controls all publication rights for the U.S.A. and Canada

COOL GROOVE

Now try playing half notes in 3/4 time.

Copyright © 2012 by HAL LEONARD CORPORATION

An **eighth note** lasts half a beat, or half as long as a quarter note. One eighth note is written with a stem and flag; consecutive eighth notes are connected with a beam.

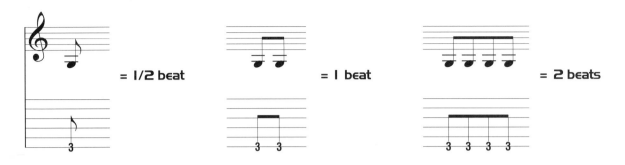

LADY MADONNA

While playing this Beatles classic, count with the word "and" between the beats.

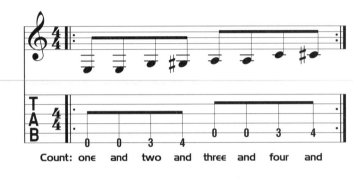

CRAZY TRAIN

Randy Rhoads played the driving, eighth-note guitar riff on this immortal Ozzy Osbourne song.

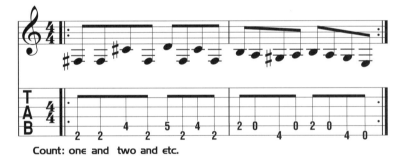

AQUALUNG

Now let's mix eighth notes and quarter notes on this famous Jethro Tull song.

GREEN-EYED LADY

Experiment to determine which fingers work best for this classic Sugarloaf riff. Just be sure to use your fingertips; don't play "flat-fingered."

A **rest** is a symbol used to indicate silence in music. In 4/4 time, a **quarter rest** fills the time of one beat and a **half rest** fills the time of two beats.

25 OR 6 TO 4

This riff by the band Chicago uses a quarter rest. Mute the string by touching it gently with the palm of your picking hand. You can also release the pressure of your fret hand to silence the string.

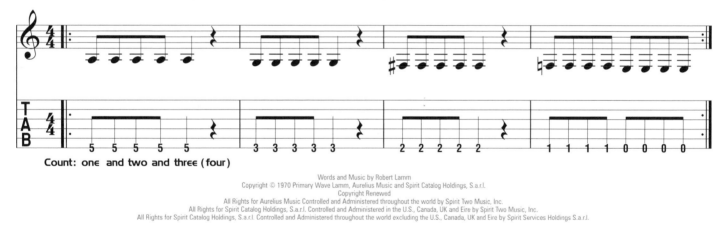

BRAIN STEW

The band Green Day used a similar descending pattern for this hit song, which uses quarter and half rests.

THE D STRING

Here are the notes within the first five frets of the 4th string, called the D string.

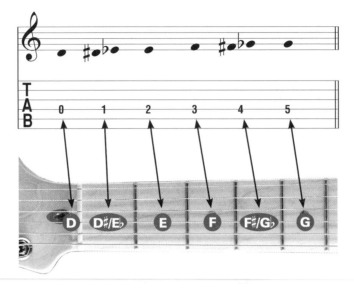

🔊 D-MENTED

Say the note names aloud as you play this sinister riff.

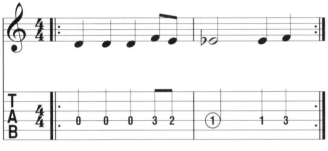

Copyright © 2012 by HAL LEONARD CORPORATION

MACHINE GUN

Jimi Hendrix used this riff as the foundation for his song from the album *Band of Gypsys*. The dot below beat 3 is called a **staccato** mark. It tells you to cut the note short.

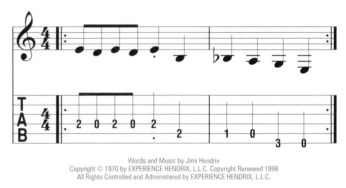

Words and Music by Jimi Hendrix
Copyright © 1970 by EXPERIENCE HENDRIX, L.L.C. Copyright Renewed 1998
All Rights Controlled and Administered by EXPERIENCE HENDRIX, L.L.C.

OH, PRETTY WOMAN

This Roy Orbison song features one of the most recognizable riffs of all time.

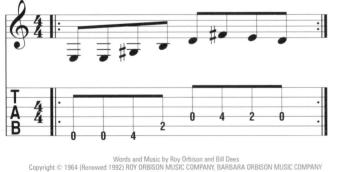

Words and Music by Roy Orbison and Bill Dees
Copyright © 1964 (Renewed 1992) ROY ORBISON MUSIC COMPANY, BARBARA ORBISON MUSIC COMPANY
and SONY/ATV MUSIC PUBLISHING LLC
All Rights on behalf of ROY ORBISON MUSIC COMPANY and BARBARA ORBISON MUSIC COMPANY
Administered by BMG CHRYSALIS
All Rights on behalf of SONY/ATV MUSIC PUBLISHING LLC Administered by SONY/ATV MUSIC PUBLISHING LLC,
8 Music Square West, Nashville, TN 37203

YOU GIVE LOVE A BAD NAME

As you play this Bon Jovi riff, use the side or heel of your pick hand to muffle the strings. This technique is called **palm muting** (P.M.).

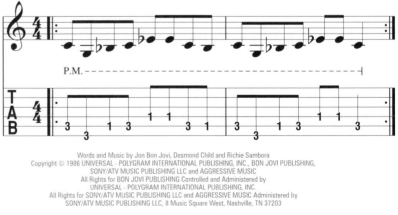

Words and Music by Jon Bon Jovi, Desmond Child and Richie Sambora
Copyright © 1986 UNIVERSAL - POLYGRAM INTERNATIONAL PUBLISHING, INC., BON JOVI PUBLISHING,
SONY/ATV MUSIC PUBLISHING LLC and AGGRESSIVE MUSIC
All Rights for BON JOVI PUBLISHING Controlled and Administered by
UNIVERSAL - POLYGRAM INTERNATIONAL PUBLISHING, INC.
All Rights for SONY/ATV MUSIC PUBLISHING LLC and AGGRESSIVE MUSIC Administered by
SONY/ATV MUSIC PUBLISHING LLC, 8 Music Square West, Nashville, TN 37203

A **tie** is a curved, dashed line connecting two notes of the same pitch. It tells you not to strike the second note. The first note should be struck and held for the combined value of both notes.

| Two Beats | Three Beats | One Beat |

SPACE TRUCKIN'

You're now ready to tackle this driving riff from the band Deep Purple.

MONEY (THAT'S WHAT I WANT)

"Money" has been recorded by countless artists, including Barrett Strong, the Beatles, Buddy Guy, and Waylon Jennings.

An **eighth rest** indicates to be silent for half a beat. It looks like this: ⅞

🔊 HAVA NAGILA

Start slowly and use your pinky for the G♯ on the 4th fret.

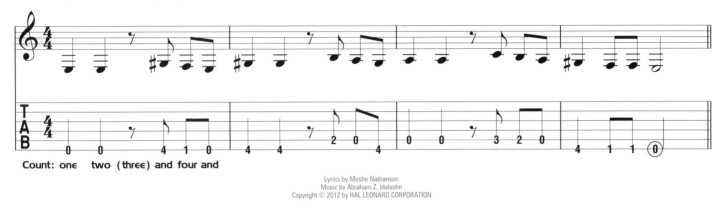

Count: one   two (three) and four and

SUPER FREAK

This funky Rick James hit uses both eighth and quarter rests.

JAMIE'S CRYIN'

This Van Halen riff uses both eighth rests and ties.

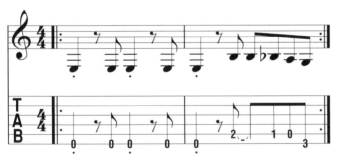

DAY TRIPPER

On this Beatles classic, you'll get a workout on all three bottom strings.

The next riffs begin with **pickup notes**. Count pickup notes as if they were the last portion of a full measure.

YOU REALLY GOT ME
Van Halen covered this Kinks song on their first album.

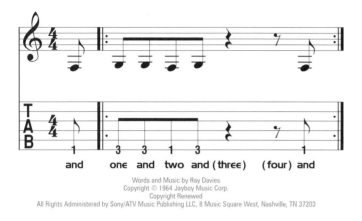

and   one   and   two   and (three)   (four) and

MISSISSIPPI QUEEN
A wavy line over a note indicates to apply **vibrato**, a technique produced by pulling (bending) and releasing a string in rapid succession.

COME AS YOU ARE
This Nirvana riff begins on the "and" of beat 3.

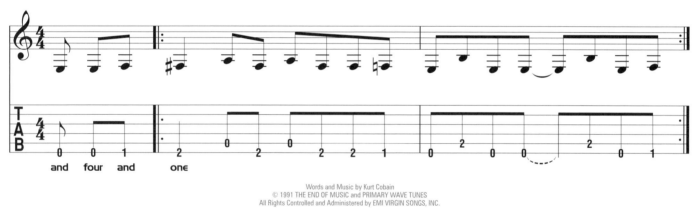

and   four   and   one

FEEL YOUR LOVE TONIGHT
Here's another Van Halen riff. This one applies palm muting and vibrato.

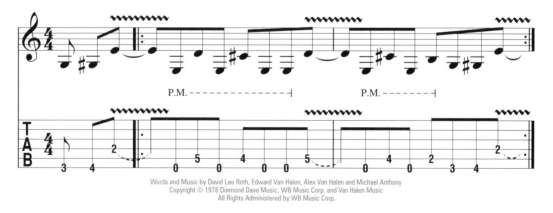

🔊 WIPE OUT

Now it's time to play your first complete song. "Wipe Out" is one of the most popular instrumental hits of all time. It was originally recorded by the Surfaris in 1963 and has been performed since by numerous groups, including the Ventures and the Beach Boys.

During the famous drum breakdown in the second half of the song, you'll notice a **whole rest**. It indicates one full measure of silence, and looks like this: ▬

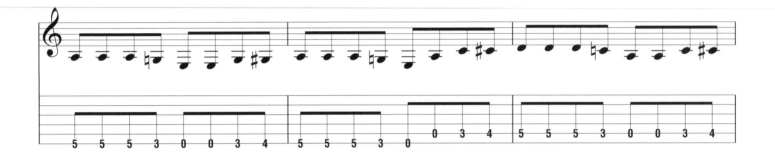

By The Surfaris
© 1963 (Renewed) MIRALESTE MUSIC and ROBIN HOOD MUSIC CO.

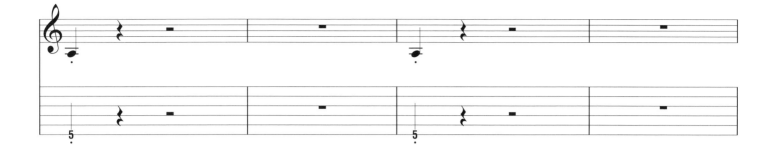

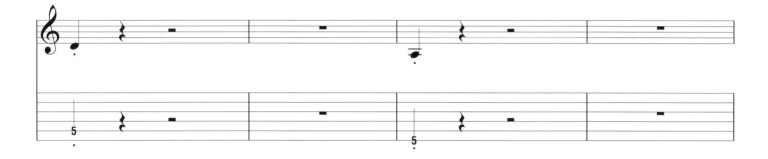

CHECKPOINT

You have completed Chapter 1 of this book and are well on your way to a rewarding hobby or a successful career with the guitar. Let's take a moment to review some of what you've learned so far.

NOTE NAMES

Draw a line to match each note on the left with its correct name on the right.

SYMBOLS & TERMS

Draw a line to match each symbol on the left with its correct name on the right.

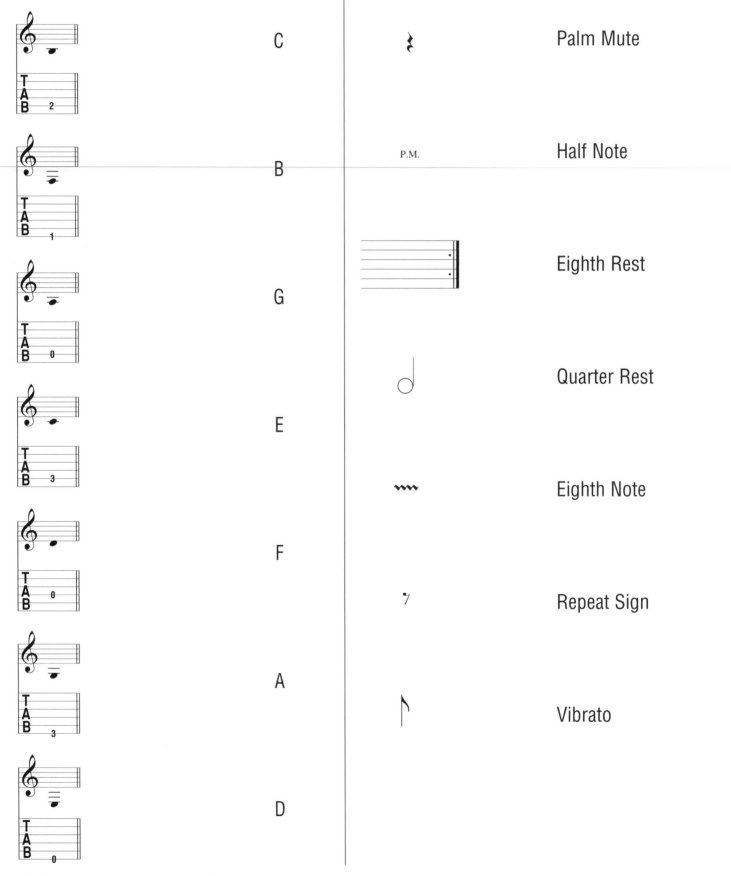

Write the note names in the spaces provided.

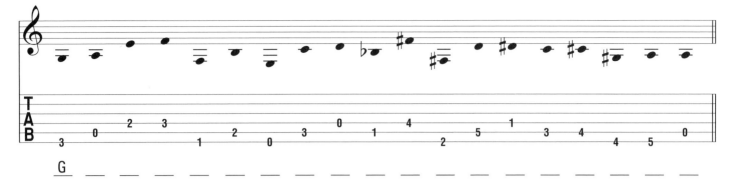

G _ _ _ _ _ _ _ _ _ _ _ _ _ _ _ _ _

Add bar lines.

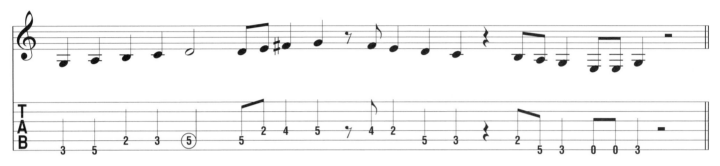

Below the tab staff are note names. Write the notes on the tab staff.

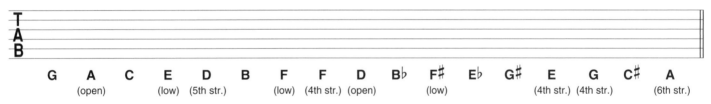

G	A	C	E	D	B	F	F	D	B♭	F♯	E♭	G♯	E	G	C♯	A
(open)	(low)	(5th str.)		(low)	(4th str.)	(open)		(low)					(4th str.)	(4th str.)		(6th str.)

CHAPTER 2
POWER CHORDS

A **power chord** consists of two notes played together. Rock guitarists use power chords to create a low, powerful sound.

The lower note of a power chord is called the **root note**. It is the note upon which the chord is named. The power chord label also includes the suffix "5."

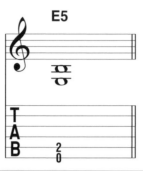

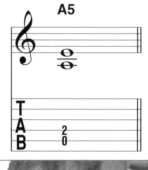

🔊 METALLIC

Attack both notes of the power chord at the same time with a single downstroke.

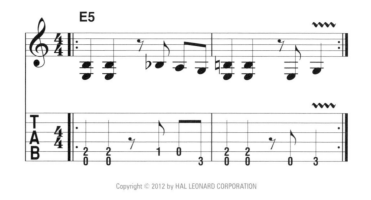

🔊 JACK HAMMER

Remember to stop the chords from ringing when you see rests or staccato dots.

T.N.T.

Australian hard rock band AC/DC uses power chords in many songs, including this classic riff from "T.N.T."

Words and Music by Angus Young, Malcolm Young and Bon Scott

MOVABLE POWER CHORDS

Power chords can be played up and down the lower strings of the guitar fretboard using one simple fingering shape. Use your 1st and 3rd fingers as shown below.

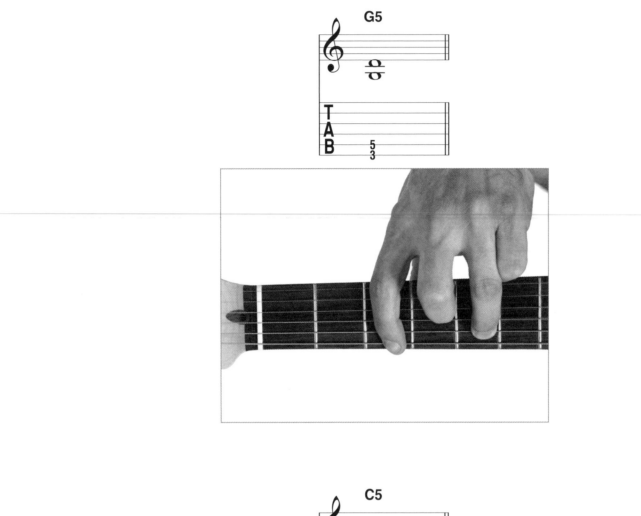

A power chord's name comes from its root note, or where your 1st finger is placed on the fretboard. Here is a diagram of the notes you've learned so far within the first five frets of strings 5 and 6, and the power chords built upon these roots.

ROOT ON 6TH STRING

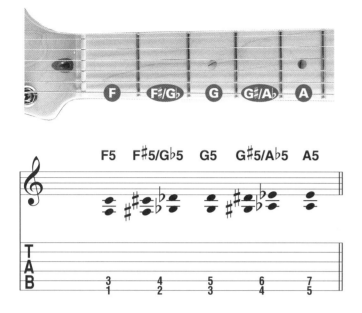

ROOT ON 5TH STRING

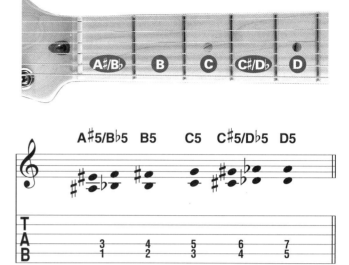

ALL ALONG THE WATCHTOWER

Bob Dylan, Jimi Hendrix, and others have recorded this song. The root note of all three power chords is on the 6th string.

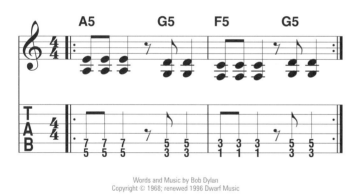

MEGA-HEAVY

This riff chugs on the low E string between power chord attacks.

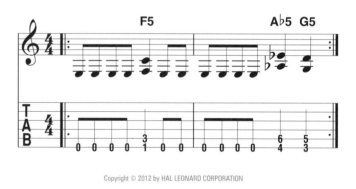

SMELLS LIKE TEEN SPIRIT

This Nirvana hit uses power chords with roots on the 5th and 6th strings.

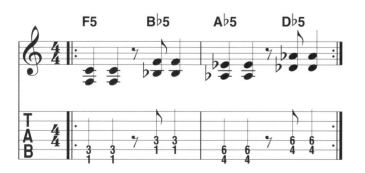

I CAN'T EXPLAIN

Guitarist Pete Townshend of the Who used power chords in many songs, including "I Can't Explain."

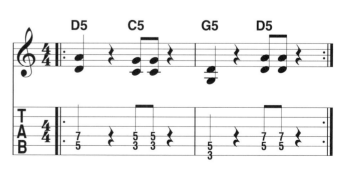

When a **dot** appears after a note, you extend the note by half its value. A **dotted half note** lasts for three beats.

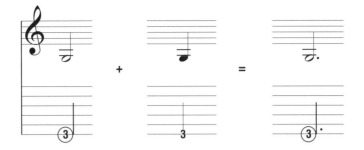

A **whole note** is twice as long as a half note; it lasts four beats. A whole note is written in a circle with no stem.

BABA O'RILEY

Now let's mix movable and open power chords to play another rock classic by the Who.

REFUGEE

Tom Petty's "Refugee" also puts power chords and single notes to good use.

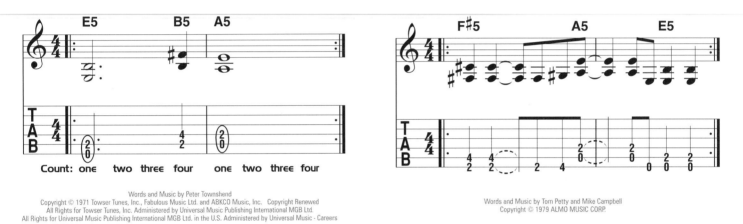

BATMAN THEME

Here's an easy, fun riff that is a variation of the open A5 power chord.

JAILBREAK

Power chords are often mixed with single notes. Try this riff popularized by the band Thin Lizzy.

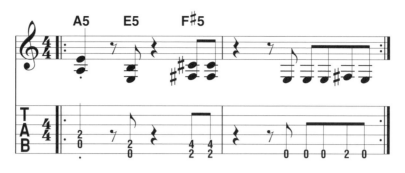

OWNER OF A LONELY HEART

This riff by the band Yes is tabbed with **ending brackets**. The 1st time through, play the 1st ending and repeat as usual. The 2nd time, skip the 1st ending and play the 2nd ending.

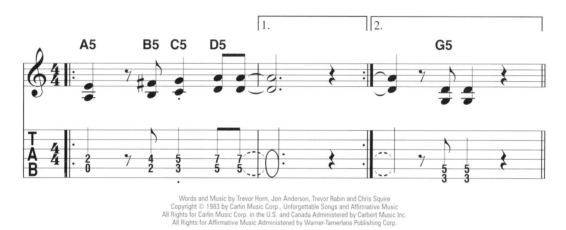

🔊 CHICAGO BLUES

Blues guitarists commonly enhance simple power chords in a manner similar to this rhythm figure.

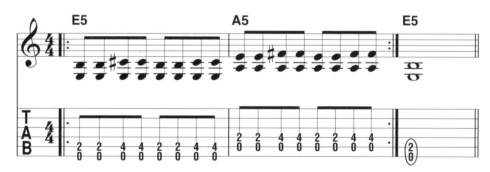

🔊 WILD THING

"Wild Thing" is one of rock music's most enduring songs. Originally a #1 hit for the Troggs in 1966, it has since been recorded by Jimi Hendrix, Sam Kinison, and many others. The entire song can be played using movable power chords.

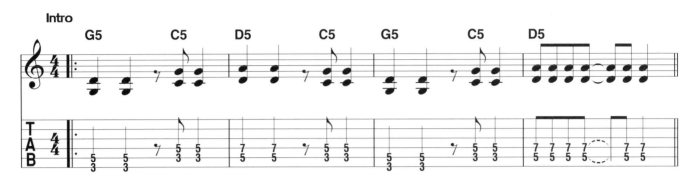

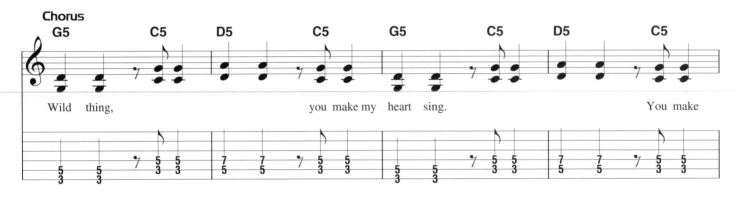

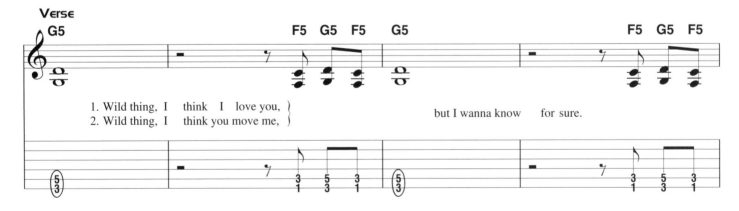

Words and Music by Chip Taylor
© 1965 (Renewed 1993) EMI BLACKWOOD MUSIC INC.

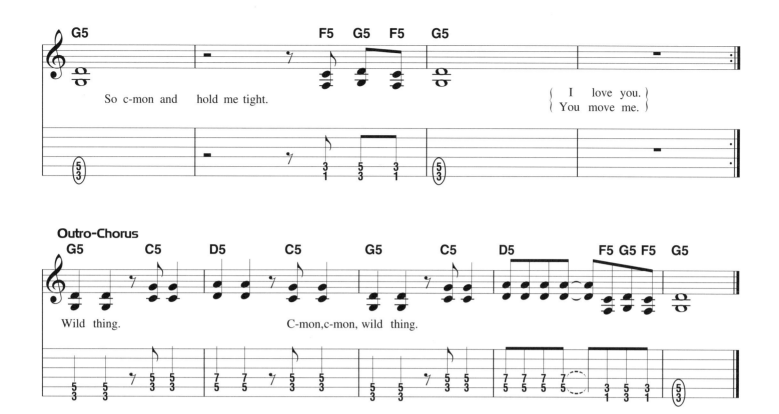

THE G STRING

Here are the notes within the first five frets of the 3rd string, called the G string.

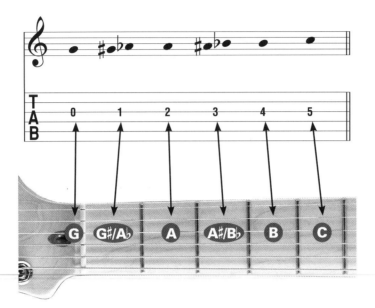

NORWEGIAN WOOD (THIS BIRD HAS FLOWN)

This Indian-influenced Beatles song, written in 3/4 time, was the first rock song to feature a sitar on a recording.

DON'T FEAR THE REAPER

In some songs, like this cowbell-infused classic by Blue Öyster Cult, it's common to see the instruction "**let ring**." Instead of releasing your fingers after each note is played, you hold them down, allowing the notes to sustain.

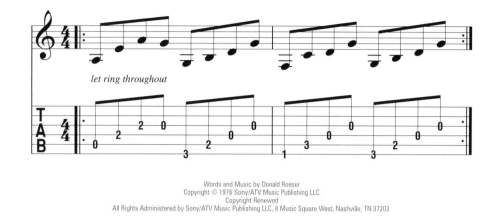

LA BAMBA

This song has been recorded by Ritchie Valens, Los Lobos, and many others. It uses notes on all four strings you've learned so far. Use your 2nd finger to press the notes on the 2nd fret and 3rd finger on the 3rd fret.

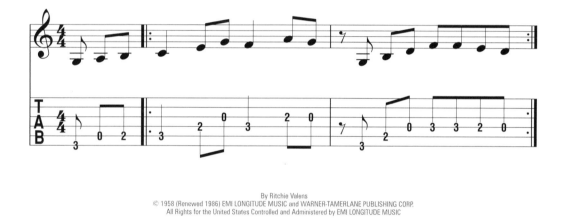

SMOKE ON THE WATER

Deep Purple's "Smoke on the Water" features one of the greatest rock riffs of all time. Strike the two-note chords, or **dyads**, with downstrokes. Although you haven't learned notes beyond the 5th fret, simply use your 3rd finger to press the notes on the 6th fret.

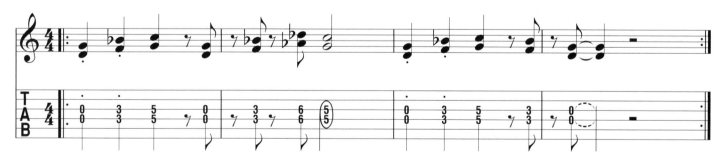

PIPELINE

"Pipeline" is a classic guitar instrumental. The original version was a surf-rock hit for the Chantays in 1963, and it has since been recorded by the Ventures, Dick Dale, Stevie Ray Vaughan, and others. It uses single notes on the bottom four strings, as well as a few power chords. In the A section, fret the B note (5th string, 2nd fret) for the entire four measures.

Repeat previous measure

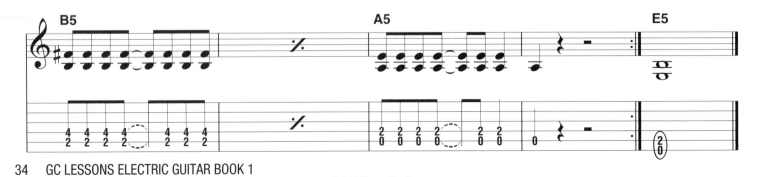

By Bob Spickard and Brian Carman
Copyright © 1962, 1963 (Renewed) by Regent Music Corporation (BMI)

THE B STRING

Here are the notes within the first five frets of the 2nd string, called the B string.

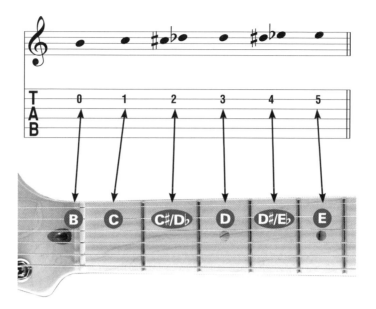

DUELIN' BANJOS

This bluegrass theme was featured in the movie *Deliverance.*

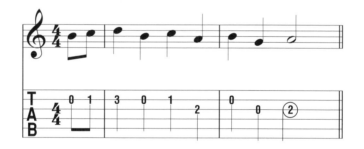

By Arthur Smith
© 1955, 1974 (Renewed 1983, 2002) TEMI COMBINE INC.
All Rights Controlled by COMBINE MUSIC CORP. and Administered by EMI BLACKWOOD MUSIC INC.

SUSIE-Q

Creedence Clearwater Revival covered this Dale Hawkins song on their first album.

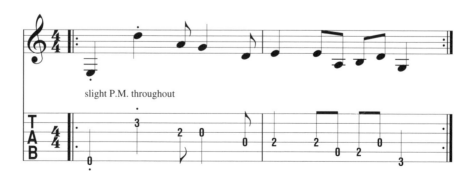

Words and Music by Dale Hawkins, Stan Lewis and Eleanor Broadwater
Copyright © 1957 (Renewed) by Arc Music Corp. (BMI)
Arc Music Corp. Administered by BMG Chrysalis for the world excluding Japan and Southeast Asia

FÜR ELISE

This instantly recognizable piece in 3/4 time is truly a classic. Beethoven wrote it in 1810.

By Ludwig van Beethoven
Copyright © 2012 by HAL LEONARD CORPORATION

WALK DON'T RUN

The Ventures, Chet Atkins, and others have recorded this popular instrumental song.

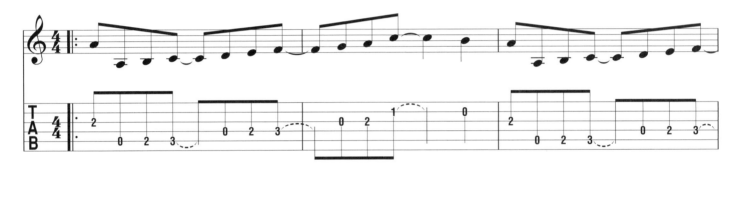

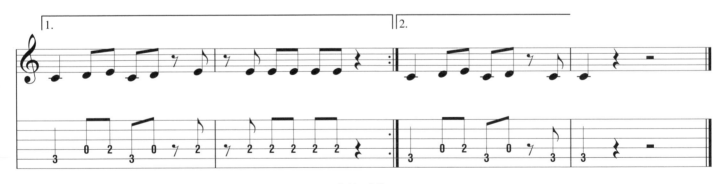

By Johnny Smith
Copyright © 1960 by Peermusic Ltd., On Board Music and Mesa Verde Music Co.
Copyright Renewed
All Rights Administered by Peermusic Ltd.

THE HIGH E STRING

Here are the notes within the first five frets of the 1st string, called the E string.

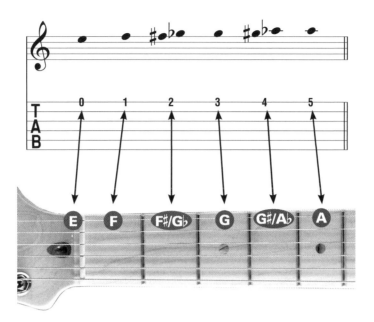

IN MY LIFE

The opening riff of this song by the Beatles uses notes on the top two strings. Fret-hand fingerings are indicated below the tab staff.

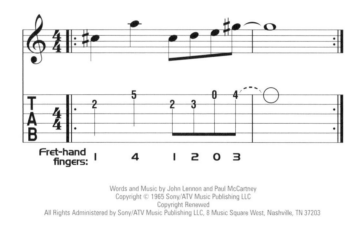

TICKET TO RIDE

Here's another classic intro by the Beatles. Keep your 1st finger planted on the first note and let the strings ring throughout.

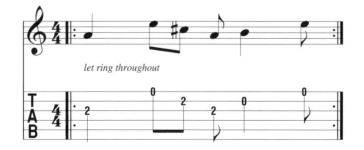

REBEL, REBEL

To play this David Bowie riff, follow the "let ring" indications and be sure to mute the low E note in the 2nd measure with your palm.

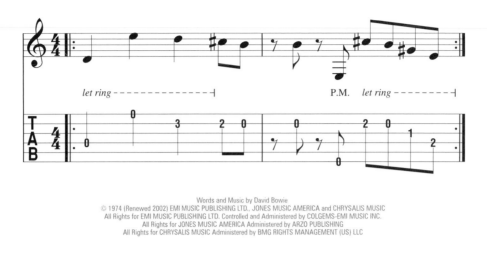

SUNDAY BLOODY SUNDAY

Now play this riff by the band U2, paying close attention to the fingerings below the tab. Keep the notes depressed so they ring, and lay your 1st finger across the top three strings at the 2nd fret for the last half of measure 1.

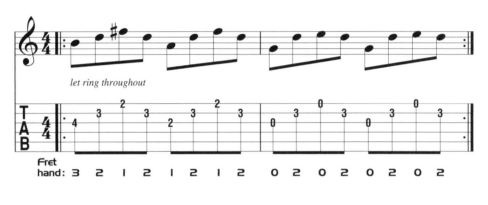

FOXEY LADY

Here is one of Jimi Hendrix's signature riffs. Lay your pinky across the top two strings to play the notes at the 5th fret.

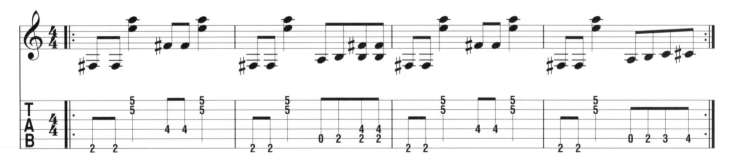

JAMES BOND THEME

The main theme of the James Bond films is powerful, mysterious, and instantly recognizable. It contains notes on all six strings, and is arranged here as a duet for two guitars. Pick a part and play! Once you've reached the end of section E, you'll see the instructions "D.S. al Coda (no repeat)." Jump back to the sign (𝄋) at letter B and play up to the instruction "To Coda." At this point, jump to the last line of the tune where it's labeled "Coda," and play the final five measures.

C

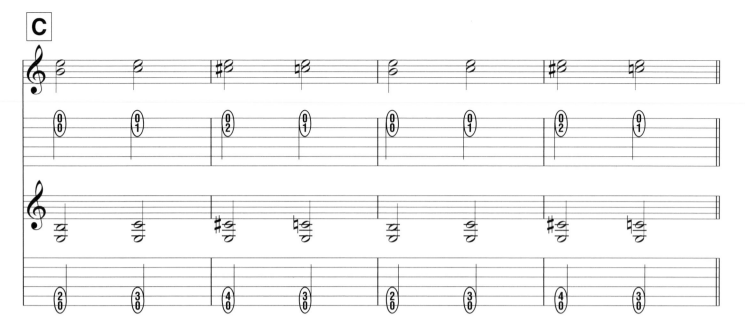

D

Jump back to
the sign (𝄋) ↘

D.S. al Coda
(no repeat)

𝄌 **Coda**

CHECKPOINT

Congratulations, you've reached the end of Chapter 2. Let's review some of what you've learned.

NOTE NAMES

Draw a line to match each note on the left with its correct name on the right.

SYMBOLS & TERMS

Draw a line to match each symbol on the left with its correct name on the right.

Write the note names in the spaces provided.

Add bar lines.

CHAPTER 3
OPEN CHORDS

Chords that contain open strings are called open-position chords, or simply **open chords**. They are used for accompaniment, or **rhythm guitar**, and usually incorporate four, five, or all six strings.

Em

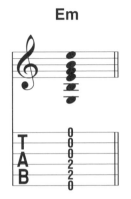

D

GET UP STAND UP

Playing chords in a rhythmic pattern is called **strumming**. Strum the E minor chord in a downward motion to play a basic version of this Bob Marley song.

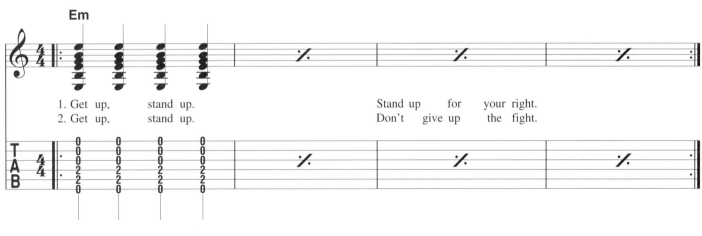

1. Get up,   stand up.   Stand up   for   your right.
2. Get up,   stand up.   Don't   give up   the fight.

Words and Music by Bob Marley and Peter Tosh
Copyright © 1974 Fifty-Six Hope Road Music Ltd., Odnil Music Ltd., State One Music America LLC and Embassy Music Corporation
Copyright Renewed
All Rights in North America Administered by Blue Mountain Music Ltd./Irish Town Songs (ASCAP) and throughout the rest of the world by Blue Mountain Music Ltd. (PRS)

LAND OF A THOUSAND DANCES

Now try the D chord for this Wilson Pickett classic. Arch your fingers and play on the tips to avoid touching the other strings.

Na, na, na, na, na, na, na, na, na, na, na, na, na, na, na.

HEART OF GOLD

Let's practice changing between two chords with the intro from one of Neil Young's greatest hits.

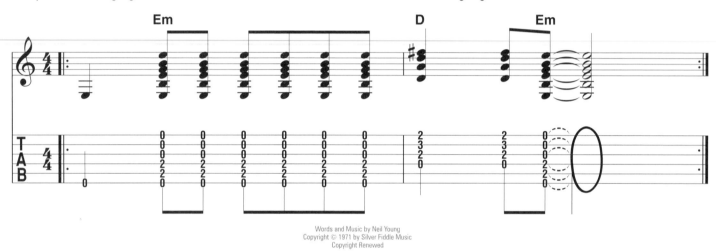

Here are two more common open chords: C and D. Try them with the songs on the next page.

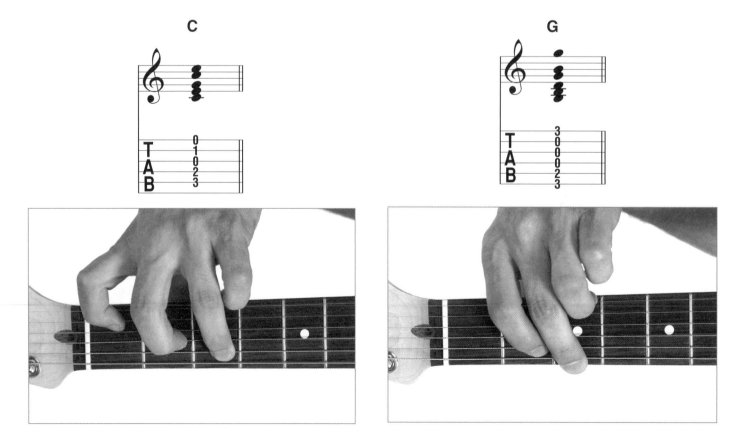

YELLOW SUBMARINE

Try to keep a steady strum as you change chords for this all-time Beatles favorite.

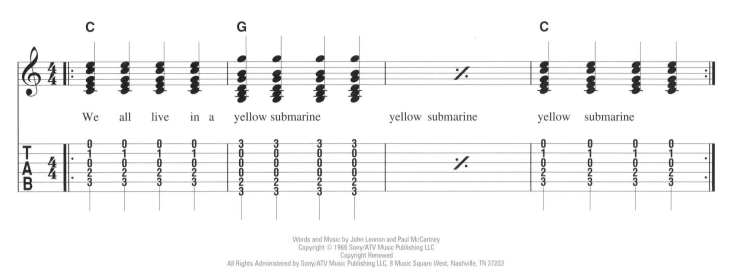

SPACE ODDITY

David Bowie used C and E minor chords at the beginning of the verse for this hit song.

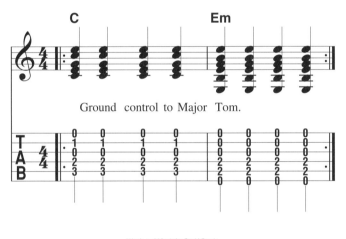

SHOULD I STAY OR SHOULD I GO

Open D and G chords kick off the intro of this classic by the Clash.

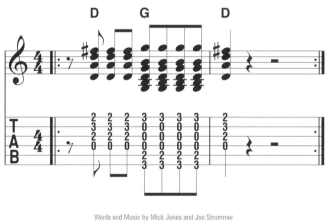

WONDERFUL TONIGHT

For Eric Clapton's "Wonderful Tonight," let's try a new strum pattern that uses both downstrokes (⊓) and upstrokes (∨).

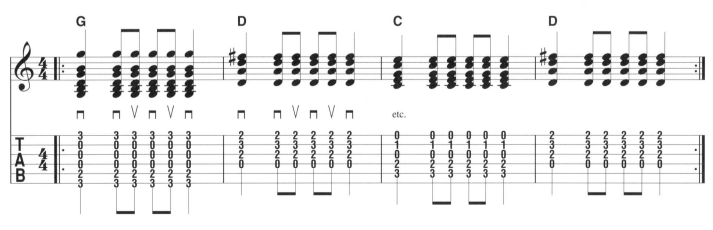

WILD NIGHT

Van Morrison's "Wild Night" is a certified rock classic and has been covered by numerous artists. It uses all four open chords introduced so far. Play the strum patterns written or feel free to try your own variations.

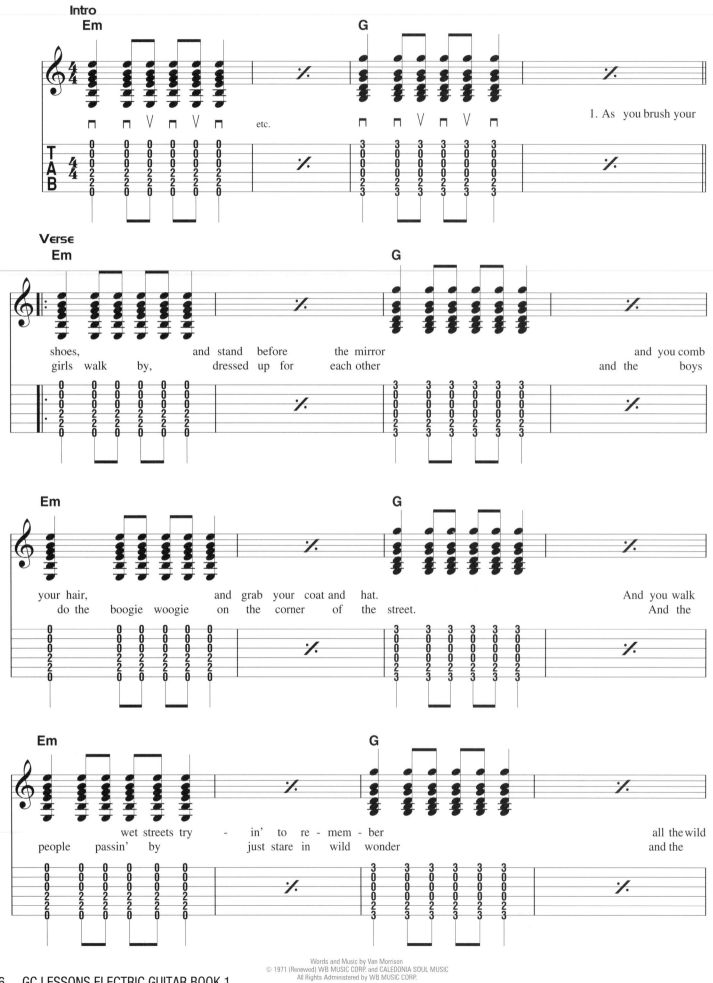

Words and Music by Van Morrison
© 1971 (Renewed) WB MUSIC CORP. and CALEDONIA SOUL MUSIC
All Rights Administered by WB MUSIC CORP.

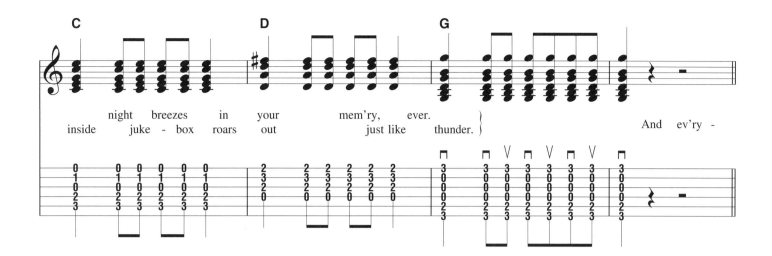

night breezes in your mem'ry, ever.
inside juke - box roars out just like thunder. And ev'ry -

Pre-Chorus

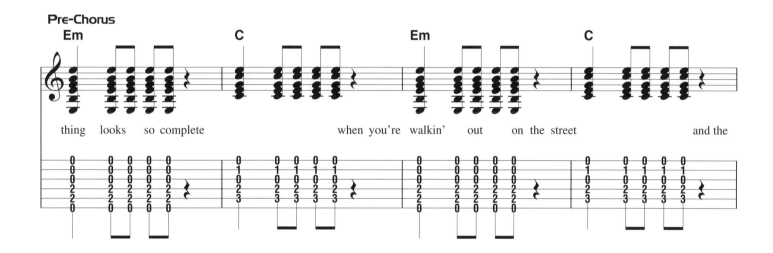

thing looks so complete when you're walkin' out on the street and the

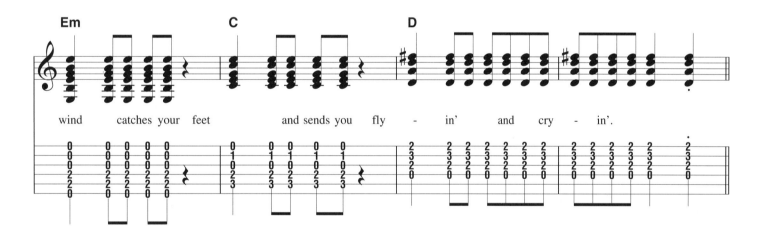

wind catches your feet and sends you fly - in' and cry - in'.

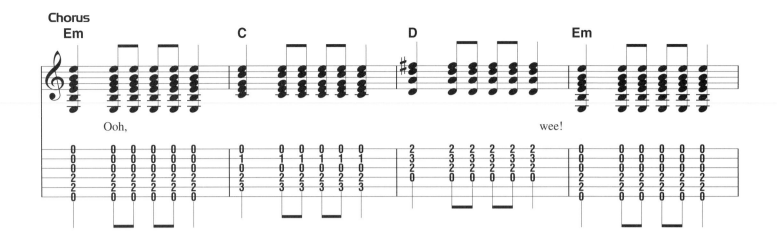

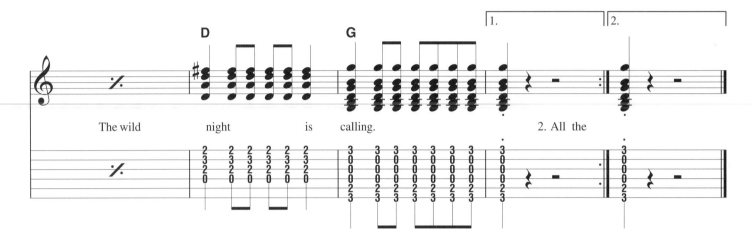

Am

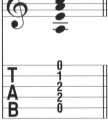

Dm

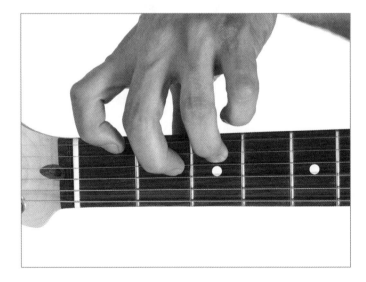

EVIL WAYS

Let's give your new A minor chord a workout with one of Santana's greatest hits. Use the palm of your pick hand to silence the strings during the rests.

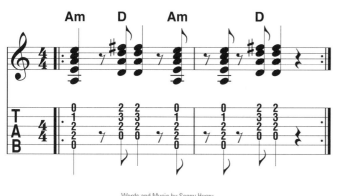

LOUIE, LOUIE

"Louie, Louie" is a rock 'n' roll standard and has been recorded by hundreds of artists. Its three-chord riff is instantly recognizable.

🔊 AIN'T NO SUNSHINE

Bill Withers' hit uses all three minor chords you've learned so far. It also incorporates two simple single notes.

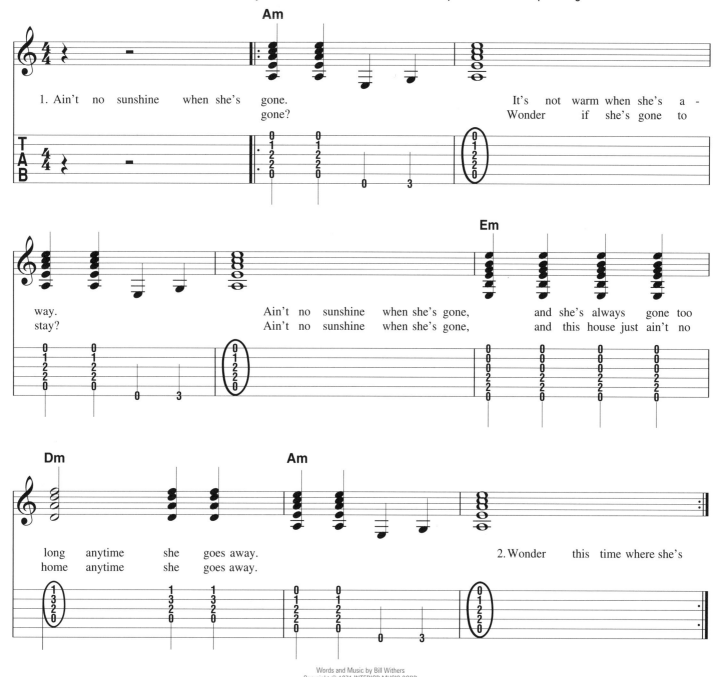

KNOCKIN' ON HEAVEN'S DOOR

Bob Dylan's timeless ballad uses open chords exclusively. Follow the strumming rhythms notated or just read the chord symbols and improvise your own strum patterns.

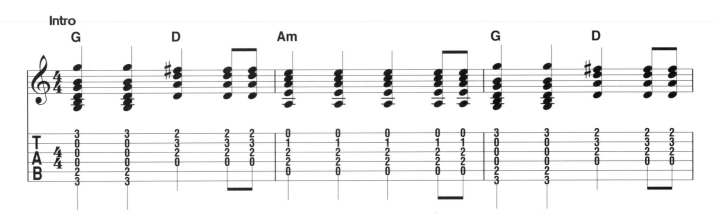

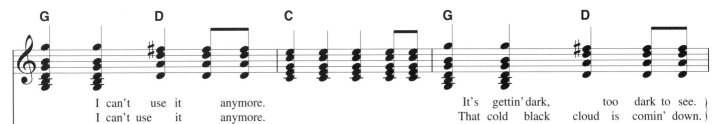

1. Mama, take   this badge   from   me.
2. Mama, put   my guns in the   ground.

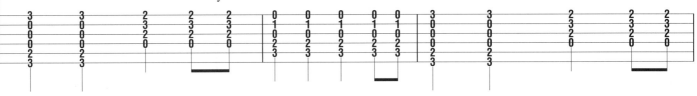

I can't   use   it   anymore.
I can't   use   it   anymore.

It's gettin' dark,   too   dark to see.)
That cold black   cloud is comin' down.)

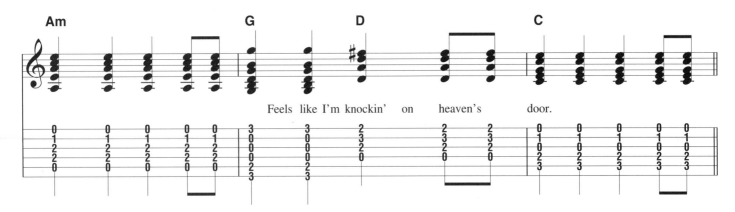

Feels like I'm knockin'   on   heaven's   door.

Words and Music by Bob Dylan
Copyright © 1973, 1974 Ram's Horn Music

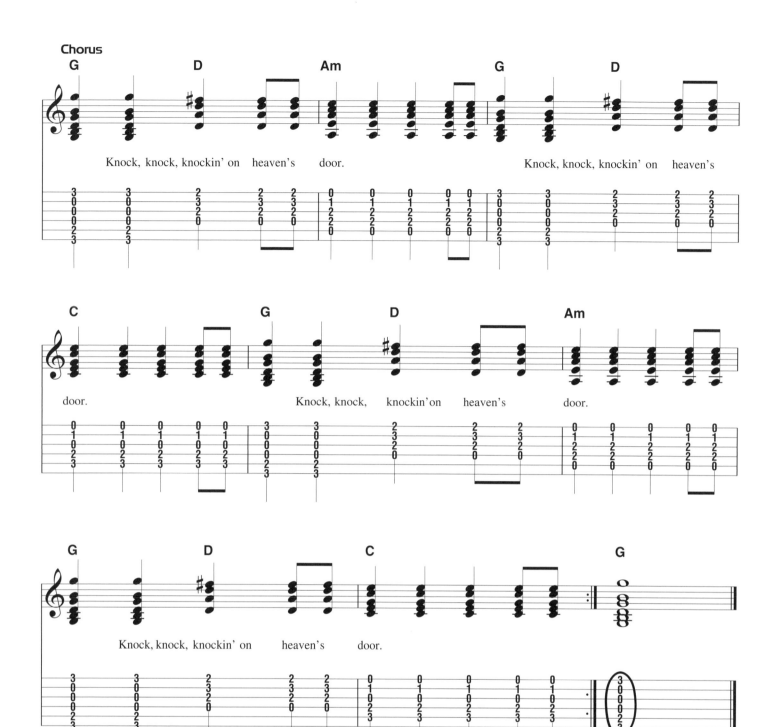

E

A

ABOUT A GIRL

For songs that change chords quickly, like this one by Nirvana, it's okay to release your fingers from one chord early in order to arrive at the next chord on time. It's natural for a few open strings to be struck in the transition.

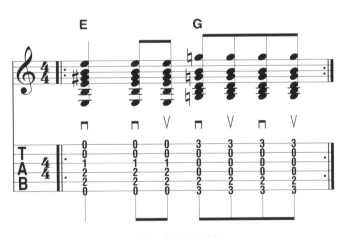

R.O.C.K. IN THE U.S.A.

When using up/down strumming, don't worry about hitting every single string on the upstroke. It's okay to just play three or four notes of the chords, or whatever feels natural.

BYE BYE LOVE

Another way to play an A chord is to lay your 1st finger across the top four strings at the 2nd fret. Many rock guitarists use this fingering and simply mute or miss the high E string. Experiment and choose which version works best for you in this hit by the Everly Brothers.

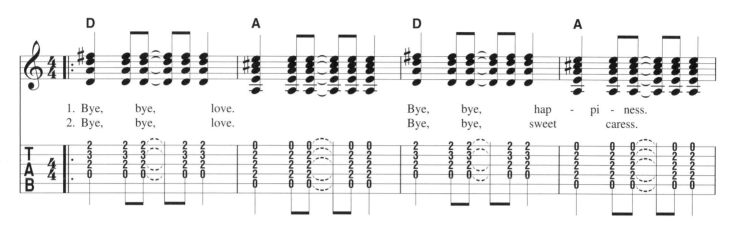

1. Bye, bye, love. Bye, bye, hap - pi - ness.
2. Bye, bye, love. Bye, bye, sweet caress.

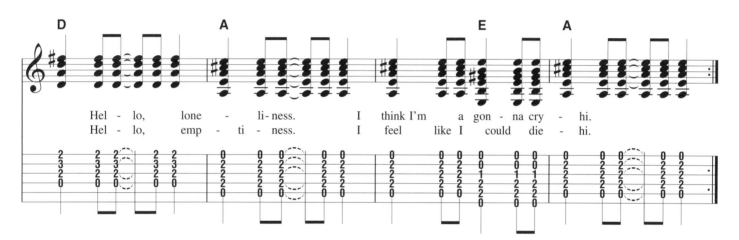

Hel - lo, lone - li - ness. I think I'm a gon - na cry - hi.
Hel - lo, emp - ti - ness. I feel like I could die - hi.

PATIENCE

Here's a hit song by Guns N' Roses that uses five open chords.

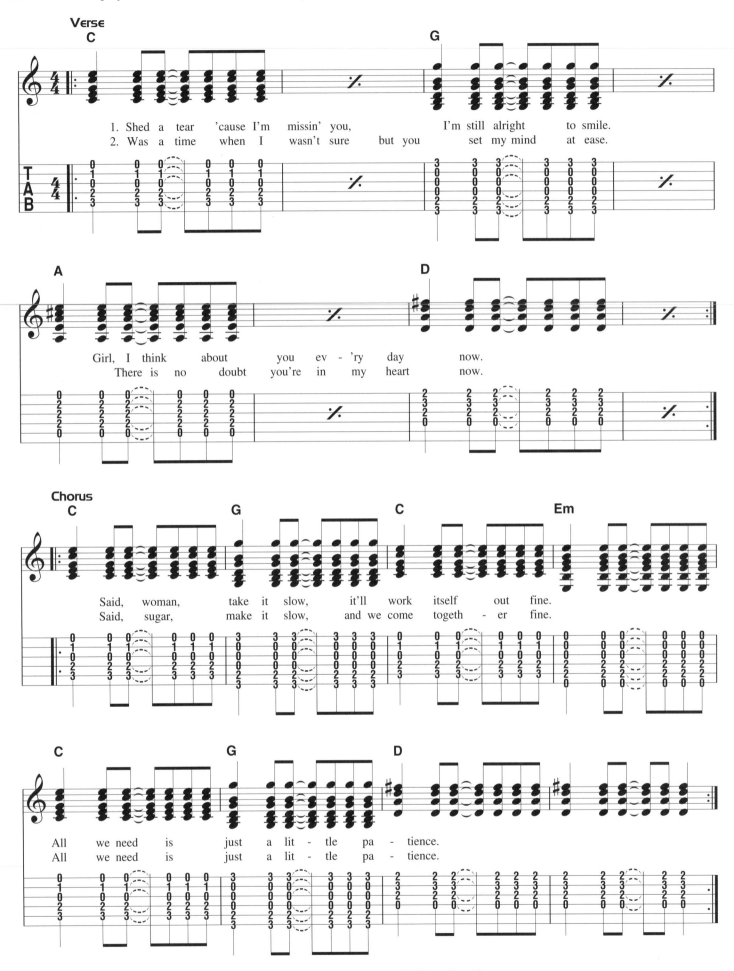

Words and Music by W. Axl Rose, Slash, Izzy Stradlin', Duff McKagan and Steven Adler
Copyright © 1988 Guns N' Roses Music (ASCAP) and Black Frog Music (ASCAP)
All Rights for Black Frog Music in the U.S. and Canada Controlled and Administered by Universal - PolyGram International Publishing, Inc.

SLIDES, HAMMER-ONS & PULL-OFFS

Sometimes, it's not so much what you play, it's how you play it. In music terms, this is called **articulation**. Slides, hammer-ons, and pull-offs all belong to a special category of articulations called **legato**. Legato techniques allow you to connect two or more consecutive notes together to create a smooth, flowing sound.

To play a **slide**, pick the first note as you normally would. Then, maintain pressure as you move your fret-hand finger up or down the fretboard to sound the second note. (The second note is not picked.) In tab, a slide is indicated with a short, slanted line and a curved **slur**.

MY SHARONA
Use your 1st finger to do the sliding for this riff by the Knack.

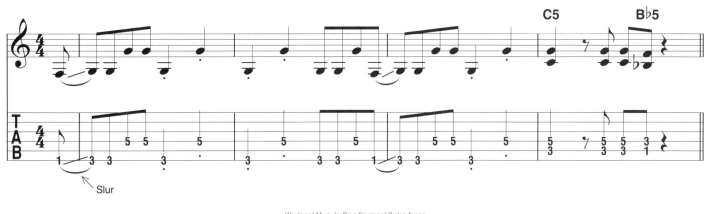

BOOM BOOM
Now try this John Lee Hooker blues riff. The slide is played with the 3rd finger. This allows your 2nd finger to play the notes on the 3rd fret and your 1st finger to play the notes on the 2nd fret.

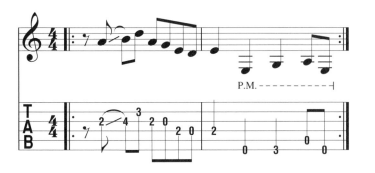

SWEET LEAF
Chords can also be connected by slides. Here is a classic heavy metal riff by the band Black Sabbath.

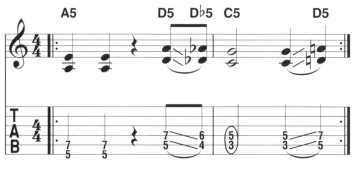

To play a **hammer-on**, pick the first note and then press down, or "hammer on" to, a higher note along the same string. The initial attack should carry the tone over both notes.

LIFE IN THE FAST LANE

Here's a famous guitar intro by the Eagles. Use your 1st finger to play the notes on the 2nd fret.

PAPERBACK WRITER

For this Beatles riff, lay your 1st finger across the bottom three strings at the 3rd fret. Maintain pressure as you use your 3rd and 4th fingers to play the notes on the 5th fret.

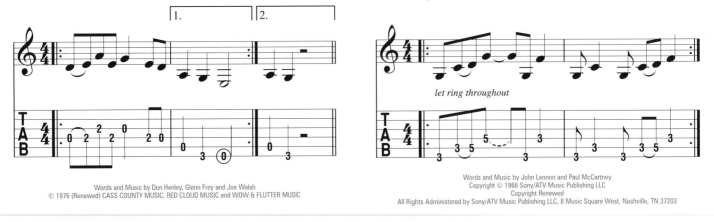

A **pull-off** is the opposite of a hammer-on. First, start with both fingers planted. Pick the higher note, then tug or "pull" that finger off the string to sound the lower note, which is already fretted by the lower finger.

BRING IT ON HOME

This riff by Led Zeppelin features pull-offs on the 3rd string.

CULT OF PERSONALITY

Notes can also be pulled off to open strings, as this riff by Living Colour demonstrates.

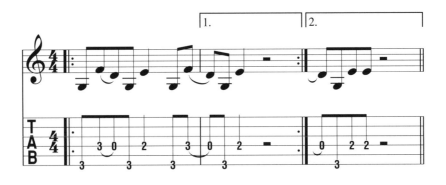

Of course, slides, hammer-ons, and pull-offs can be used in any combination. Here are a few examples.

THE MAN WHO SOLD THE WORLD

This David Bowie song was famously covered by Nirvana on MTV's *Unplugged.* For the back-to-back hammer-pull in the 2nd measure, only the first of the three notes is picked.

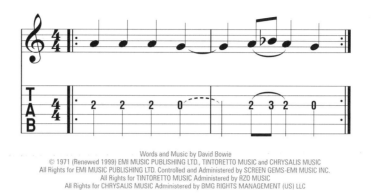

COME OUT AND PLAY

The Offspring's "Come Out and Play" contains hammer-ons and slides. The first part of the slide occurs very quickly and is called a **grace-note slide**.

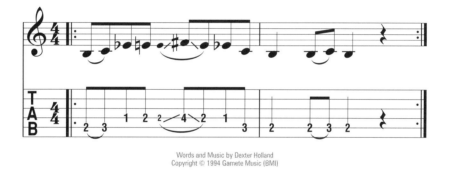

🔊 BLUEGRASS RUN

Legato articulations are common in all styles of guitar music. Here's a fun bluegrass lick that uses all three types of slurs introduced so far.

HEY JOE

What better way to wrap up this unit than with one of Jimi Hendrix's biggest hits. "Hey Joe" contains several chords, single notes on all six strings, slides, hammer-ons, and more!

Intro

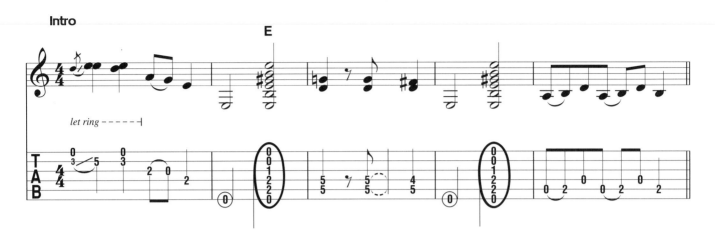

Verse

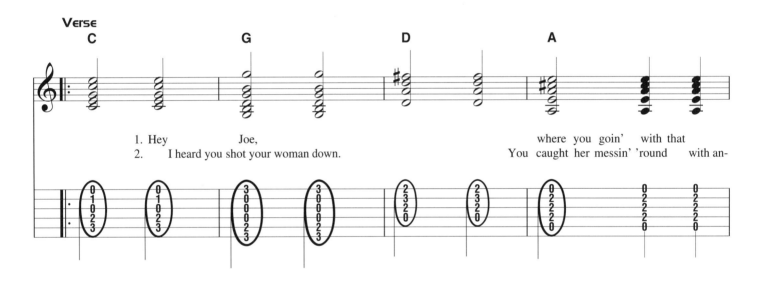

1. Hey   Joe,   where you goin'   with that
2.   I heard you shot your woman down.   You caught her messin' 'round   with an-

gun in your hand?
other   man.   And   that ain't too cool.

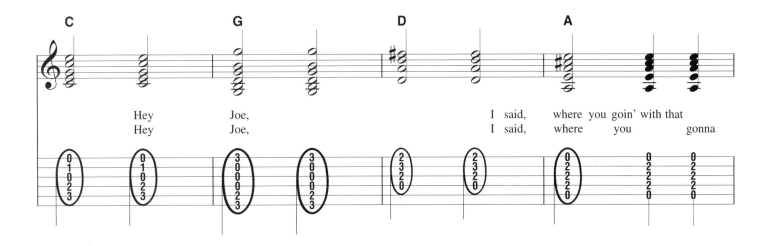

Hey   Joe,   I said,   where you goin' with that
Hey   Joe,   I said,   where   you   gonna

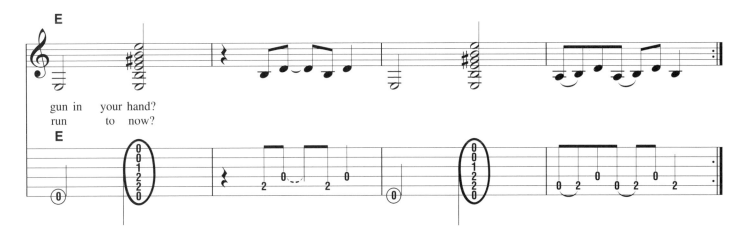

gun in   your hand?
run   to   now?

Outro

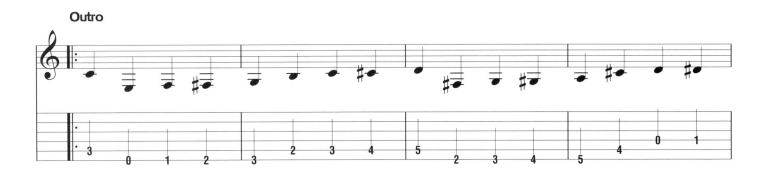

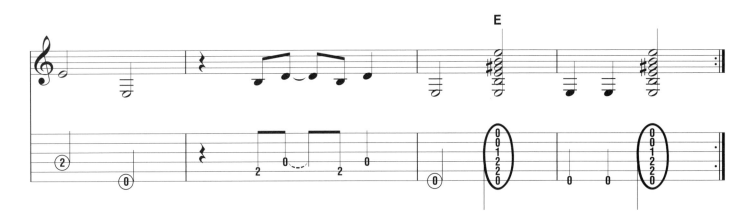

CHECKPOINT

Let's review some of what you've learned in this chapter.

CHORD NAMES

Draw a line to match each chord with its correct name.

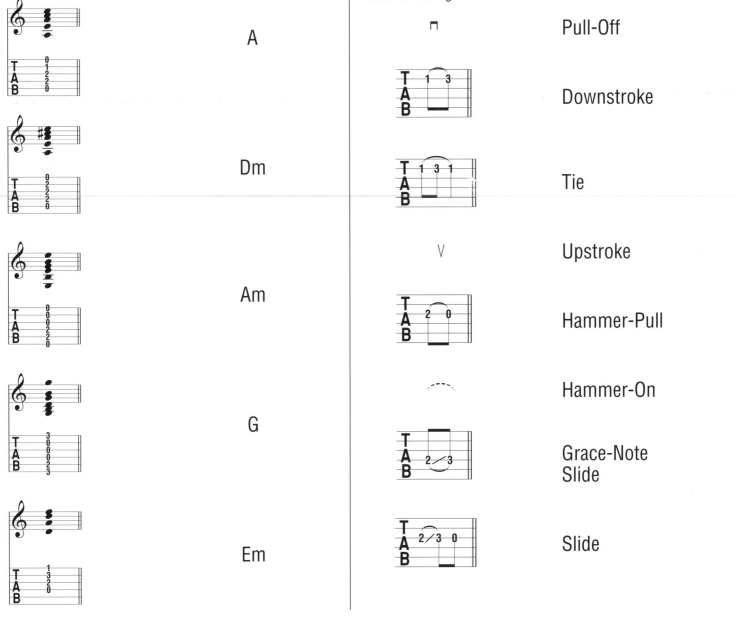

A

Dm

Am

G

Em

SYMBOLS & TERMS

Draw a line to match each symbol on the left with its correct name on the right.

Pull-Off

Downstroke

Tie

Upstroke

Hammer-Pull

Hammer-On

Grace-Note
Slide

Slide

Add bar lines.

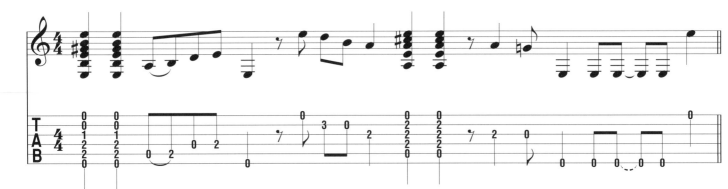

CHAPTER 4
MOVIN' UP THE FRETBOARD

In Chapters 1 and 2, we learned all of the notes within the first five frets. Now let's move beyond first position and start playing "up the neck." Here are the notes within frets 5–12 on the low three strings.

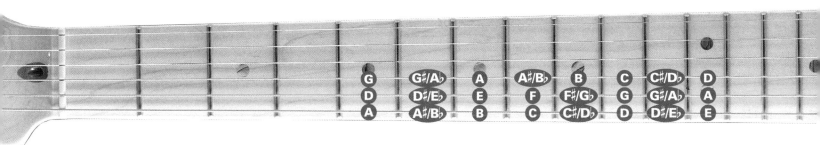

SUNSHINE OF YOUR LOVE

Eric Clapton played the immortal riff in this song with the band Cream. Use your 3rd finger to fret the first note. Then, for the final three notes, shift down two frets to use your 3rd finger (low D) and 1st finger (F).

RUNNIN' DOWN A DREAM

Use **alternate picking** to play this Tom Petty riff up to speed. This simply means to alternate between downstrokes ( ) and upstrokes ( ). For this riff, start with an upstroke.

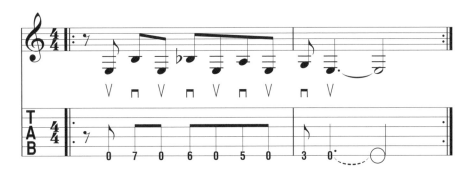

MISIRLOU

This Dick Dale surf-rock classic is fun to play on the low E string. Experiment with different fingerings, and use alternate picking to help you play more quickly. After you pick the last note, quickly slide your fret-hand finger down the string (to no particular fret).

DON'T STOP BELIEVIN'

Here's a riff by the band Journey that jumps between two areas of the fretboard. Notice that the same note can be played at different locations. The last note of the 1st measure is the same low B as the first note of the 2nd measure.

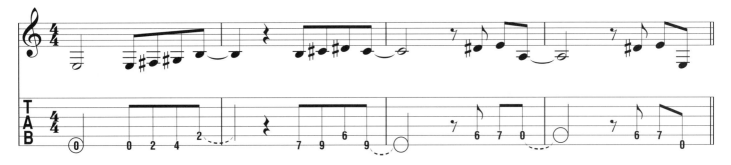

I HATE MYSELF FOR LOVING YOU

Power chords can be played "up the neck," too. The same two-finger shape is named by where the 1st finger is positioned. Here's a popular riff from the 1980s that features power chords with roots along the 5th string. Fret the 6th-string notes with your middle finger.

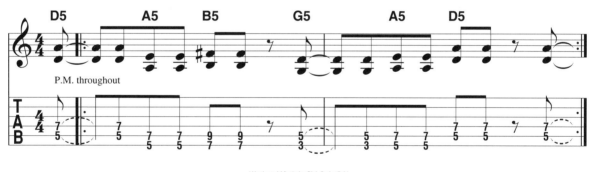

JESSIE'S GIRL

Rick Springfield's #1 hit provides more power chord practice.

ROCK YOU LIKE A HURRICANE

The German hard rock group Scorpions used power chords for this popular rock anthem.

TALK DIRTY TO ME

This famous intro by the band Poison makes use of a common rhythm guitar technique known as **muffled strings**, or "scratches." When you see X's in tab, lift your fret-hand fingers just enough to prevent the notes from sounding. A percussive, "dead" sound will then result as you pick the strings.

You've already learned that a dot after a note increases the value by one half. Therefore a **dotted quarter note** lasts for 1-1/2 beats.

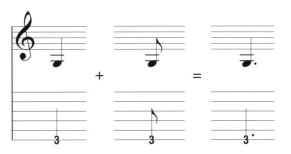

WHEREVER I MAY ROAM

Now let's mix notes and power chords all along the fretboard with hammer-ons, slides, and dotted quarter notes.

Here are the notes within frets 5–12 on the high three strings.

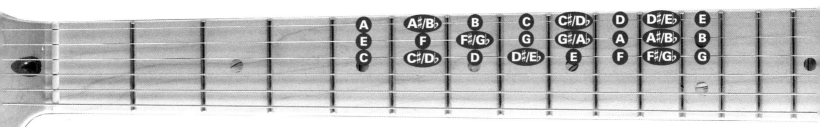

PURPLE HAZE

Jimi Hendrix's legendary riff is a must-know for all guitarists. For the first four notes, use fingers 3, 1, 2, and 1, respectively.

GET READY

This driving Motown hit makes good use of **double stops (or dyads)**, which is a term borrowed from violin technique that means to pick two notes together. Flatten your finger to depress both notes simultaneously.

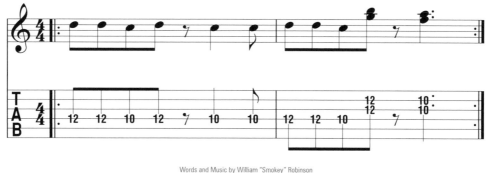

UP AROUND THE BEND

Here's a famous guitar intro by Creedence Clearwater Revival. Use your 2nd finger to play the slides and notes on the 3rd string, and lay your 1st finger across the top two strings to fret the notes at the 10th and 5th frets. Slide into the notes quickly from no particular starting point.

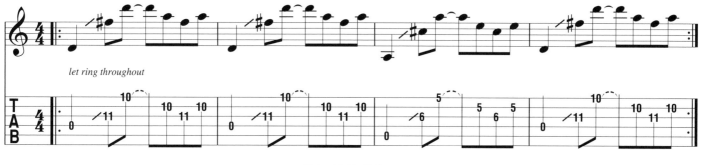

MAMA, I'M COMING HOME

Guitarist Zakk Wylde played the descending guitar riff on this Ozzy Osbourne song. Arch your fingers and play on the tips to allow the open strings to ring out.

Words and Music by Ozzy Osbourne and Zakk Wylde
© 1991 MONOWISE LTD.
All Rights for the U.S.A. and Canada Controlled and Administered by EMI VIRGIN MUSIC, INC. and EMI VIRGIN SONGS, INC.

THE MUNSTERS THEME

The sinister-sounding melody from this TV sitcom is fun to play, and provides more practice for playing "up" the neck.

By Jack Marshall
Copyright © 1973 SONGS OF UNIVERSAL, INC.
Copyright Renewed

HAWAII FIVE-O THEME

Here's another popular TV tune. It was an instrumental hit for the Ventures in 1969, and is still often heard at sporting events. This one moves quickly, so be sure to use alternate picking.

By Mort Stevens
Copyright © 1969 Sony/ATV Music Publishing LLC and Aspenfair Music
Copyright Renewed
All Rights Administered by Sony/ATV Music Publishing LLC, 8 Music Square West, Nashville, TN 37203

🔊 HE'S A PIRATE

The theme from the movie series *Pirates of the Caribbean* is played in 3/4 time. Once again, use alternate picking for the eighth notes. Also, be sure to apply vibrato when it's notated.

A

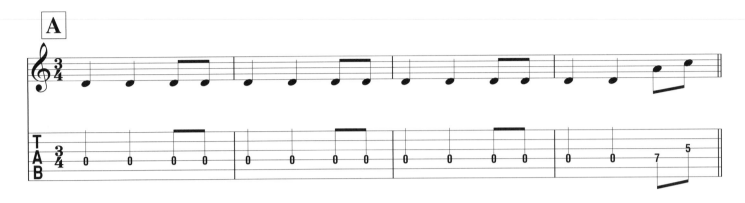

B

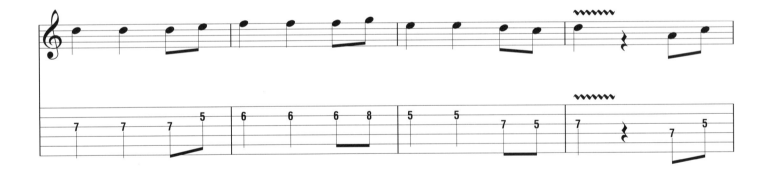

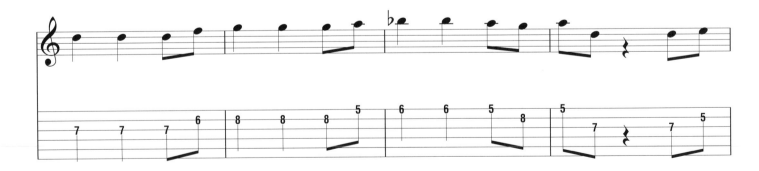

from Walt Disney Pictures' PIRATES OF THE CARIBBEAN: THE CURSE OF THE BLACK PEARL
Music by Klaus Badelt
© 2003 Walt Disney Music Company

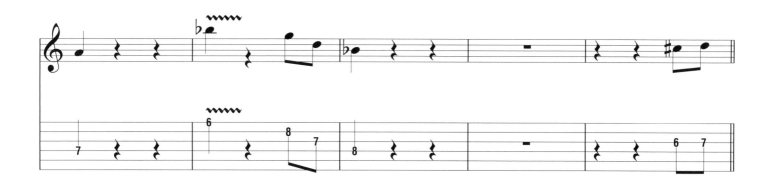

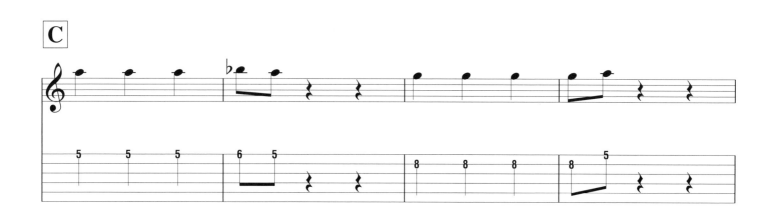

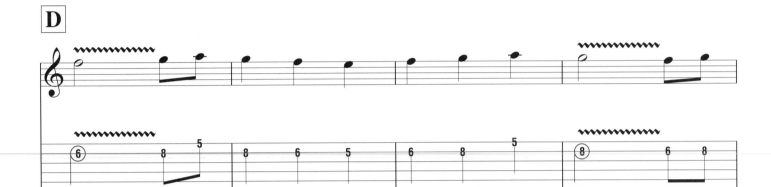

D

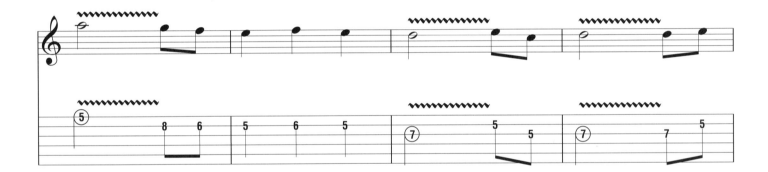

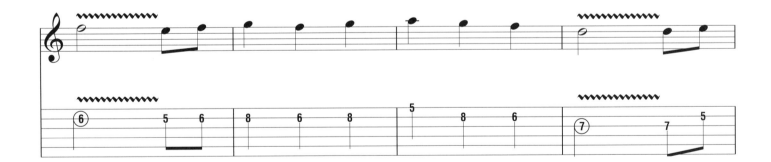

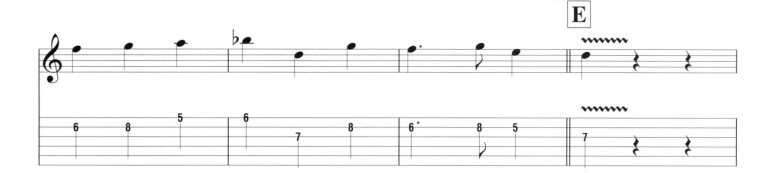

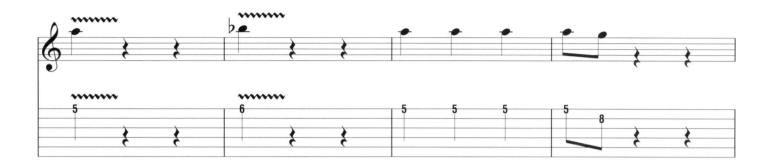

NEW RHYTHMS: ADDING SIXTEENTH NOTES

A **sixteenth note** lasts half as long as an eighth note, and is written with two flags or two beams. There are four sixteenth notes in one beat.

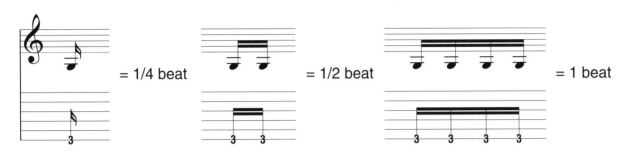

HELTER SKELTER

The raucous intro to this song by the Beatles uses sixteenth notes. Divide the beat into four, and count "one-e-and-a, two-e-and-a, three-e-and-a, four-e-and-a."

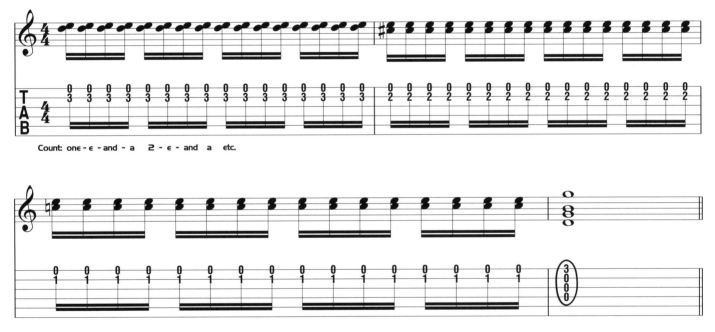

I DON'T KNOW

Ready for some faster picking? Play the sixteenth notes on the open A string using steady, alternating downstrokes and upstrokes. Also apply palm muting to sound more like the original Ozzy Osbourne recording.

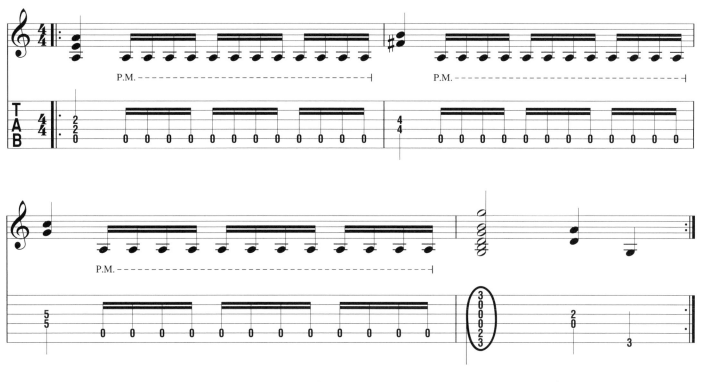

Words and Music by Ozzy Osbourne, Randy Rhoads and Bob Daisley
Copyright © 1981 Blizzard Music Limited, 12 Thayer Street, London, W1M 5LD, England

ROCK LOBSTER

Here's a fun riff by the B-52's. The second beat mixes an eighth note and two sixteenths.

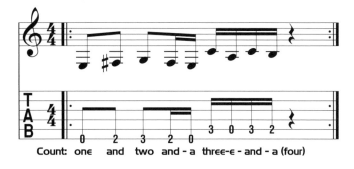

Count: one and two and - a three-e - and - a (four)

Words and Music by Kate Pierson, Fred Schneider, Keith Strickland, Cindy Wilson and Ricky Wilson
© 1979 EMI BLACKWOOD MUSIC INC., BOO FANT TUNES, INC. and DISTILLED MUSIC INC.
All Rights for BOO FANT TUNES, INC. Controlled and Administered by EMI BLACKWOOD MUSIC INC.

PLUSH

This song by Stone Temple Pilots features one of the most recognizable riffs of the 1990s.

THE TROOPER

Use pull-offs to help you play Iron Maiden's signature riff up to full speed.

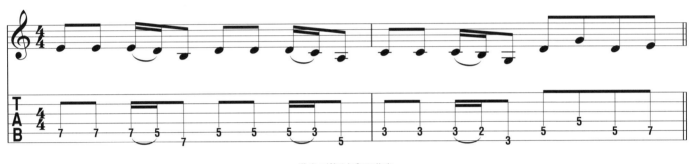

THE JOKER

This song by the Steve Miller Band was a #1 hit in 1974.

THEME FROM KING OF THE HILL

The galloping guitar riff in the theme from this animated TV series sounds cool and also serves as a great picking exercise.

from the Twentieth Century Fox Television Series KING OF THE HILL
By Roger Clyne, Brian Blush, Arthur Edwards and Paul Naffah
Copyright © 1997 T C F Music Publishing, Inc.

IRON MAN

Now let's try sixteenths with power chords in Black Sabbath's all-time classic metal track.

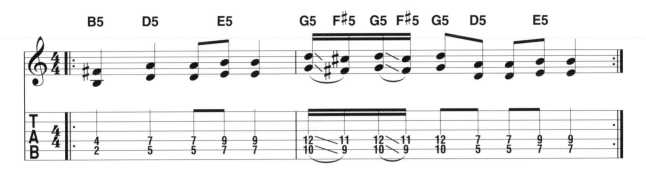

MY BEST FRIEND'S GIRL

This riff by the Cars uses muffled sixteenths in transition from the C dyad back to F.

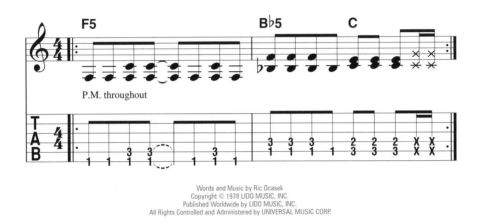

SOUTH OF HEAVEN

For a fuller sound, power chords can be expanded to three notes. Try playing the reinforced shape on this riff by the band Slayer.

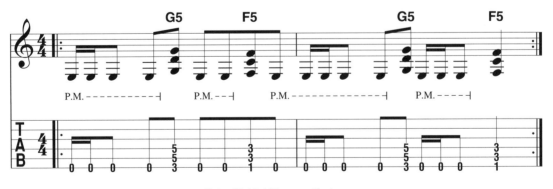

AMERICAN WOMAN

The Guess Who's #1 hit also puts three-note power chords to good use.

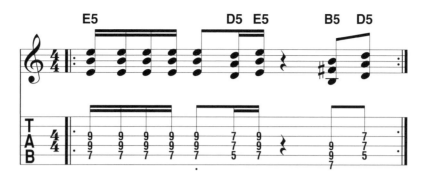

BARRACUDA

The hard rock song "Barracuda" is the band Heart's signature song. Its aggressive opening riff uses sixteenth notes and **natural harmonics**. When you see "Harm." under the tab and diamonds around the tab numbers, pick the strings while the fret-hand lightly touches the strings directly over the metal fret wire. Natural harmonics produce bell-like, chiming tones.

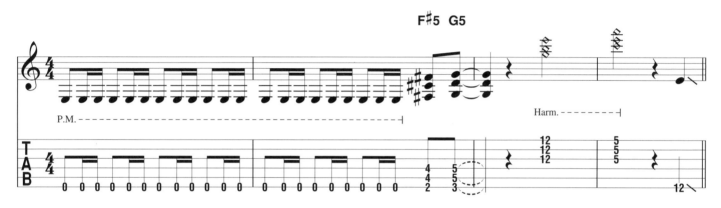

CHANGES

Jimi Hendrix recorded this song on the famous live album, *Band of Gypsys*. Two of the guitar riffs are repeated several times. To avoid tabbing the same parts over and over again, riffs and/or rhythm figures are often labeled and recalled.

Intro

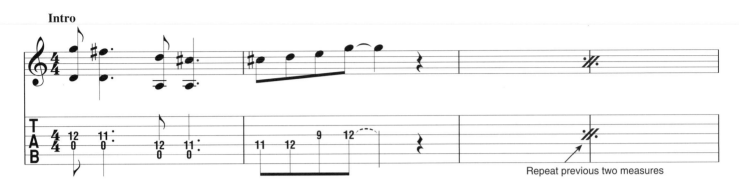

Repeat previous two measures

Riff A   **End Riff A**

Riff B   **End Riff B**

1. Well, my
2. Well, my

Verse
w/ Riff B (4 times)

mind   is goin' through them   changes,   I   feel   just   like I'm hyp - no - tized.
mind   is goin' through them   changes,   I   think I'm goin'   out of my   mind.

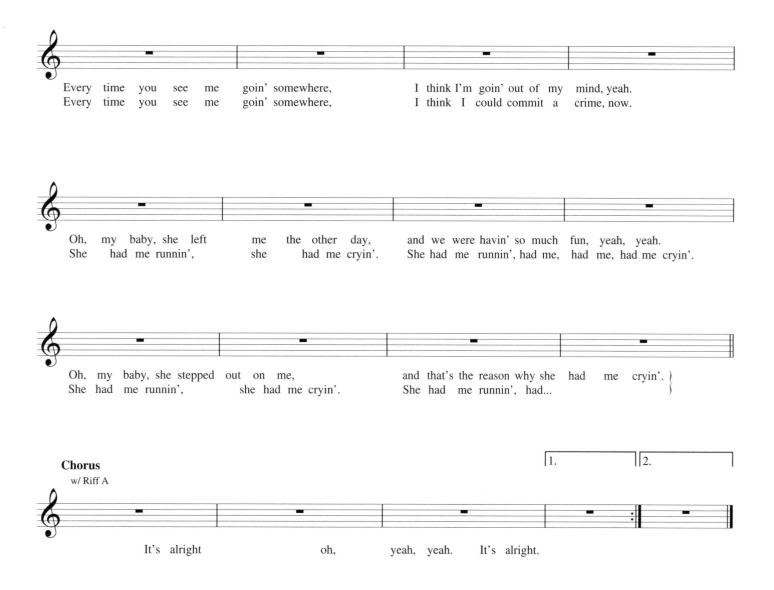

Every time you see me goin' somewhere, I think I'm goin' out of my mind, yeah.
Every time you see me goin' somewhere, I think I could commit a crime, now.

Oh, my baby, she left me the other day, and we were havin' so much fun, yeah, yeah.
She had me runnin', she had me cryin'. She had me runnin', had me, had me, had me cryin'.

Oh, my baby, she stepped out on me, and that's the reason why she had me cryin'.
She had me runnin', she had me cryin'. She had me runnin', had...

Chorus
w/ Riff A

1.   2.

It's alright oh, yeah, yeah. It's alright.

CHECKPOINT

Let's review some of what you've learned in this chapter.

NOTE NAMES

Draw a line to match each note on the left with its correct name on the right.

SYMBOLS & TERMS

Draw a line to match each symbol on the left with its correct name on the right.

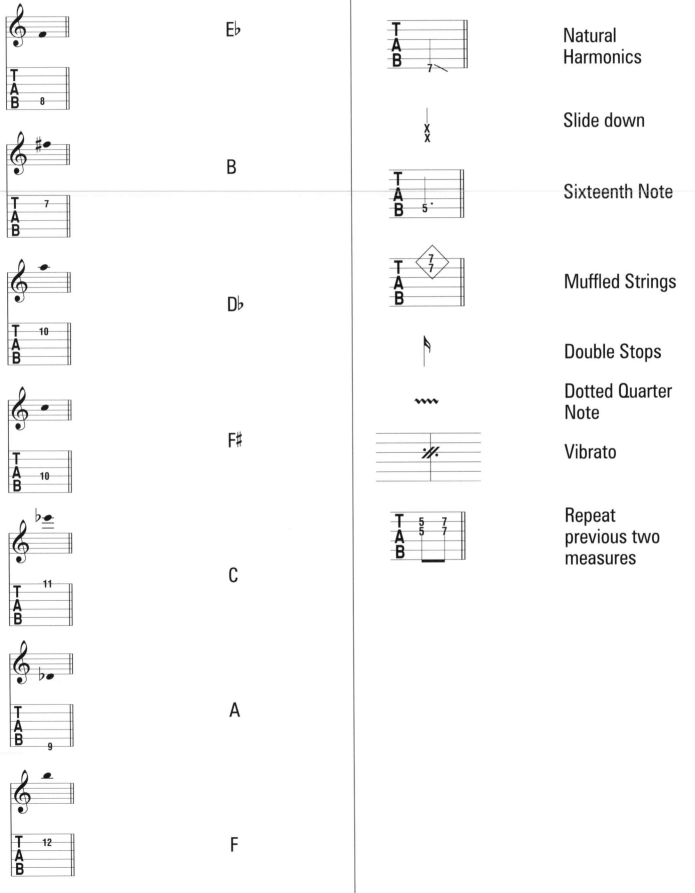

Write the note names in the spaces provided.

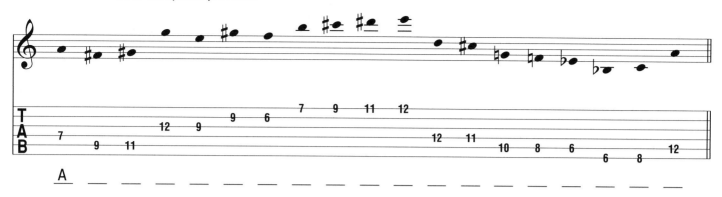

A _ _ _ _ _ _ _ _ _ _ _ _ _ _ _ _ _ _

Add bar lines.

CHAPTER 5
NEW RHYTHMS: TRIPLETS AND SHUFFLES

A **triplet** is a group of three notes played in the space of two. Whereas eighth notes divide a beat into two parts, **eighth-note triplets** divide a beat into three parts.

ADDAMS FAMILY THEME

While playing the riff from this classic TV show, count your new rhythm by simply saying the word "tri-pl-et."

Count: tri-pl-et one (two three) tri-pl-et one etc.

Theme from the TV Show and Movie
Music and Lyrics by Vic Mizzy
Copyright © 1964, Renewed 1992 by Unison Music Company
Administered by Next Decade Entertainment, Inc.

AM I EVIL?

Triplets fuel the menacing sound of this riff. Metallica's famous cover version is considered one of the heaviest metal tracks ever.

Words and Music by Sean Harris and Brian Tatler
Copyright © 1979 by Imagem London Ltd.
All Rights in the United States and Canada Administered by Universal Music - Z Tunes LLC

SPANISH BOLERO

Musicians from Maurice Ravel to Jeff Beck have made use of this rhythm. The chord movement is easy; just slide the open E chord shape.

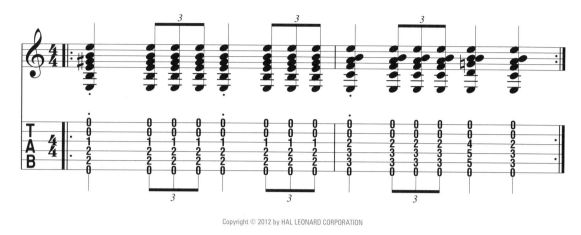

JESU, JOY OF MAN'S DESIRING

Here's a well-known classical piece that uses triplets in 3/4 time.

A **shuffle** is a bouncy, skipping rhythm. Eighth notes are played as long-short, rather than as equal values. The feel is the same as inserting a rest in the middle of a triplet.

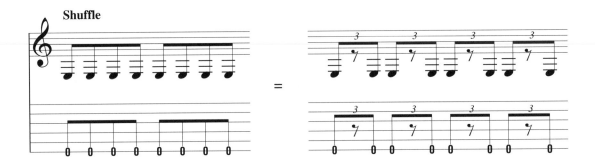

YOU SHOOK ME

Muddy Waters, Led Zeppelin, and others recorded this popular blues song.

PRIDE AND JOY

Here's the main riff of blues guitar hero Stevie Ray Vaughan's signature song. Use alternate picking.

THE BOYS ARE BACK IN TOWN

Now let's mix shuffled eighth notes and triplets to play a rock classic by Thin Lizzy.

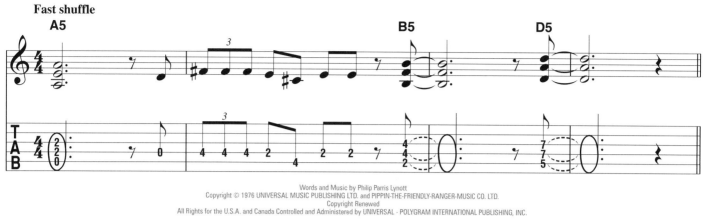

THE THAT'LL BE THE DAY

This Buddy Holly hit is one of early rock 'n' roll's most enduring songs.

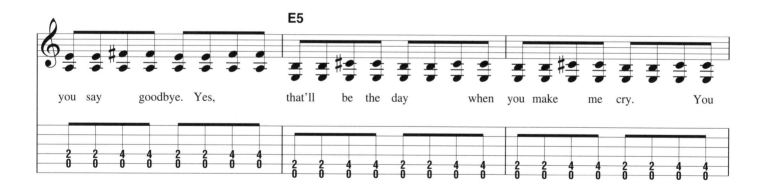

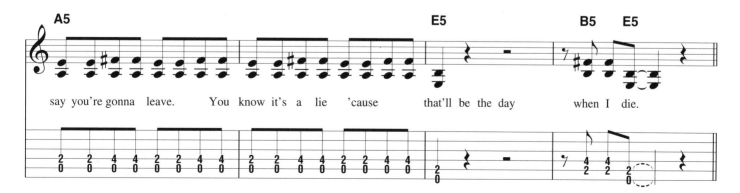

THE PINK PANTHER

Henry Mancini was one of the greatest composers of the 20th century. "The Pink Panther" is a shuffle that uses triplets, pull-offs, slides, and notes on all six strings.

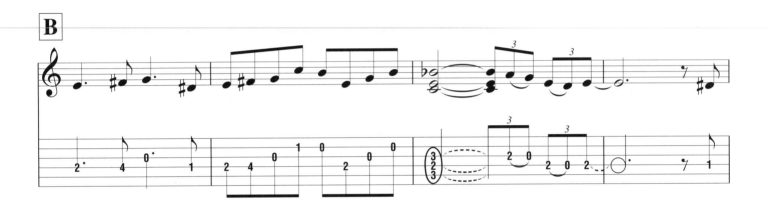

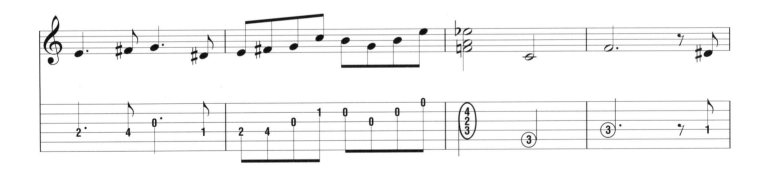

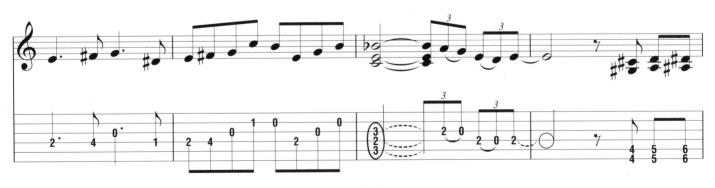

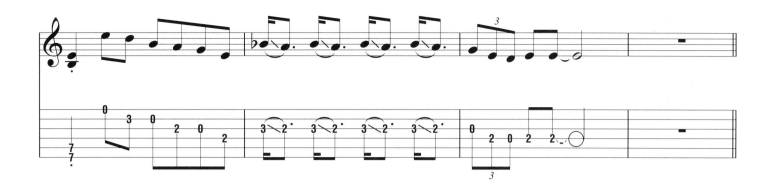

A **quarter-note triplet** divides two beats into three equal parts. In other words, the three quarter notes in this triplet equal the same time as two regular quarter notes.

= 2 beats

SEVEN NATION ARMY

Observe the counting below the tab of this riff by the White Stripes.

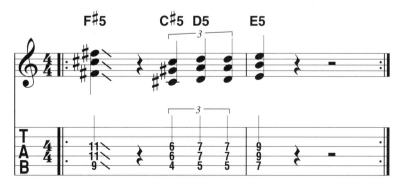

Count: one two and tri - pl - et   one two three (four)

HOLD THE LINE

The band Toto scored their first hit with "Hold the Line."

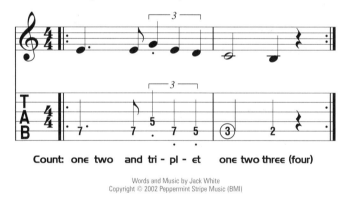

DETROIT ROCK CITY

Now try your hand at playing another full song. Here's a vintage favorite by the band Kiss.

Intro
Fast shuffle

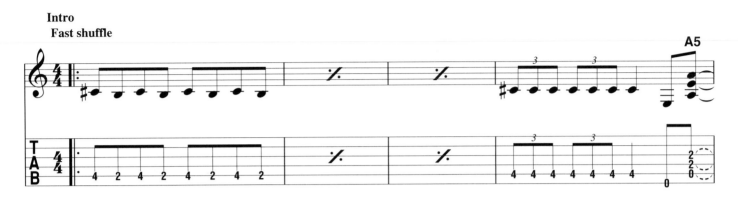

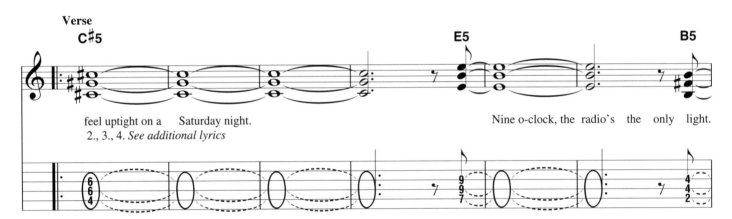

1. I

Verse

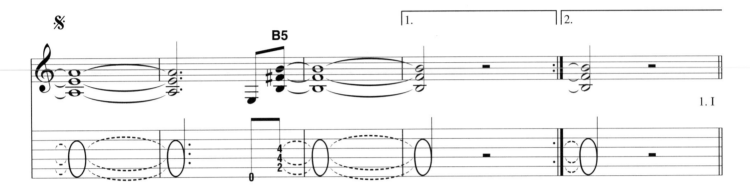

feel uptight on a   Saturday night.
2., 3., 4. *See additional lyrics*

Nine o-clock, the radio's   the   only   light.

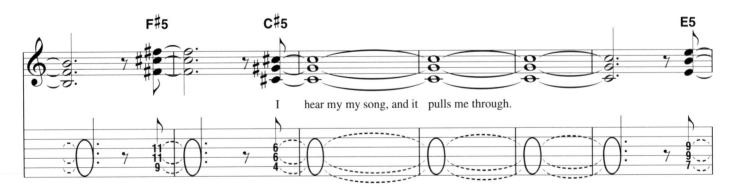

I   hear my my song, and it   pulls me through.

Words and Music by Paul Stanley and Bob Ezrin
Copyright © 1976 HORI PRODUCTIONS AMERICA, INC., ALL BY MYSELF MUSIC and CAFE AMERICANA
Copyright Renewed
All Rights for HORI PRODUCTIONS AMERICA, INC. and ALL BY MYSELF MUSIC Controlled and Administered by UNIVERSAL - POLYGRAM INTERNATIONAL PUBLISHING, INC.
All Rights for CAFE AMERICANA in the U.S. Administered by INTERSONG U.S.A., INC.
All Rights outside the U.S. excluding Japan Controlled and Administered by UNIVERSAL - POLYGRAM INTERNATIONAL PUBLISHING, INC.

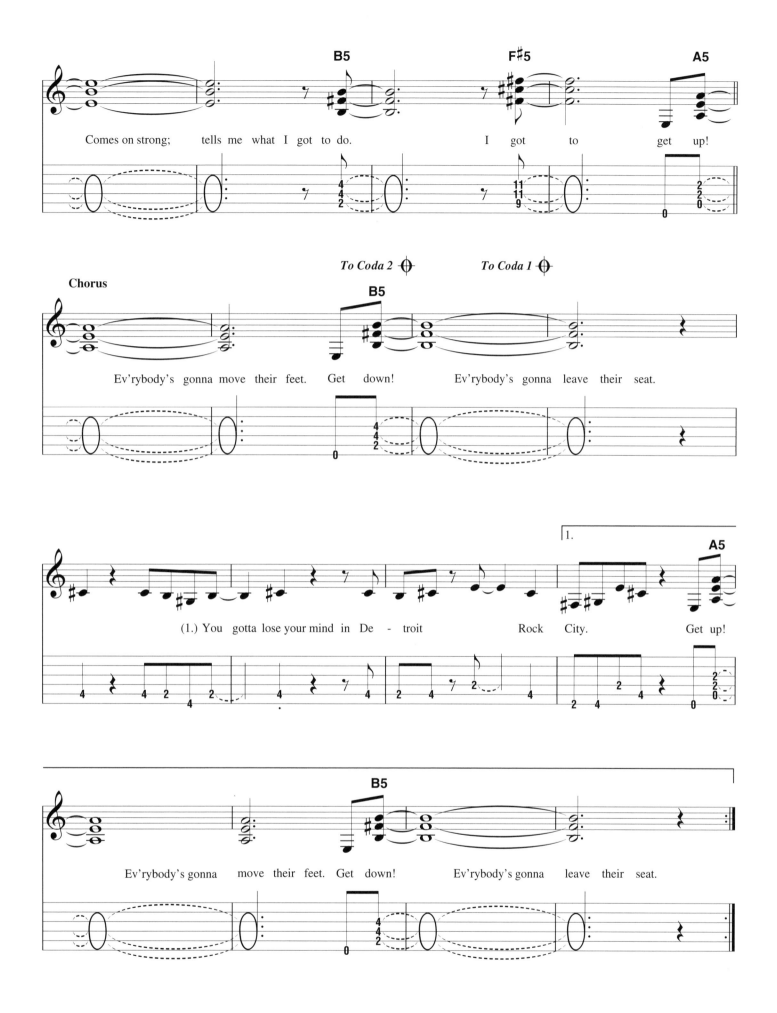

D.S. al Coda 1
(no repeat)

A5

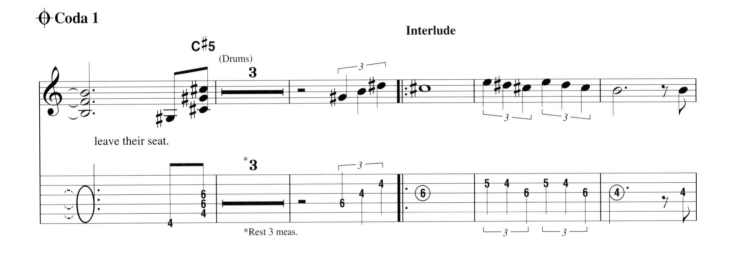

$\oplus$ **Coda 1**

C#5

(Drums)

Interlude

leave their seat.

*3

*Rest 3 meas.

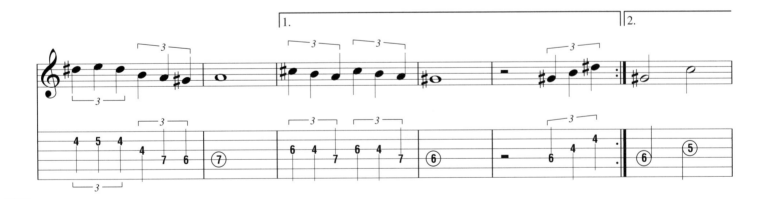

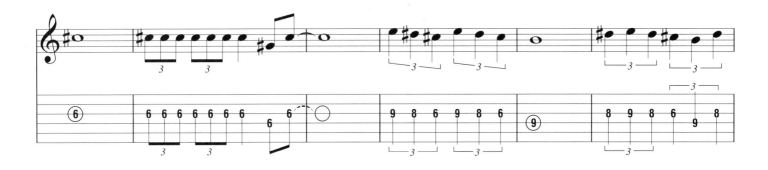

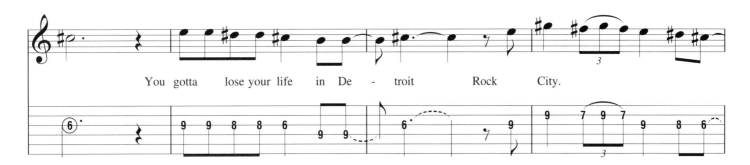

You gotta   lose your life   in De - troit   Rock   City.

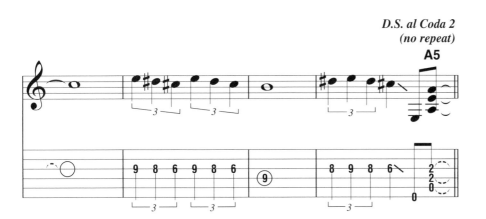

D.S. al Coda 2
(no repeat)
A5

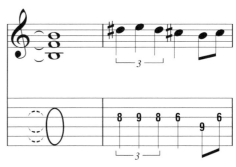
Coda 2

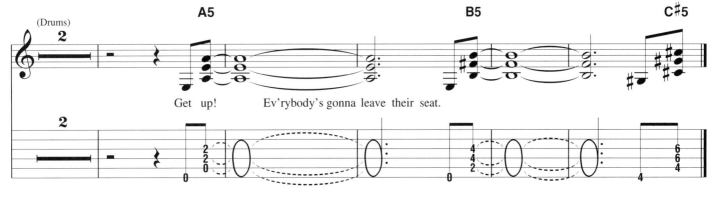

A5   **B5**   **C#5**

(Drums)

Get up!   Ev'rybody's gonna leave their seat.

Additional Lyrics

2. Gettin' late, I just can't wait.
   Ten o'clock, and I know I gotta hit the road.
   First I drink, then I smoke.
   Start up the car,
   And I try to make the midnight show. Get up!

3. Movin' fast down Ninety-Five.
   I hit top speed,
   But I'm still movin' much too slow.
   I feel so good; I'm so alive.
   Hear my song playin' on the radio.
   It goes: get up!

4. Twelve o'clock, I gotta rock.
   There's a truck ahead,
   Lights starin' at my eyes.
   Whoa, my God, no time to turn.
   I got to laugh, 'cause I know I'm gonna die.
   Why? Get up!

CHECKPOINT

Draw a line to match each rhythm with its correct name.

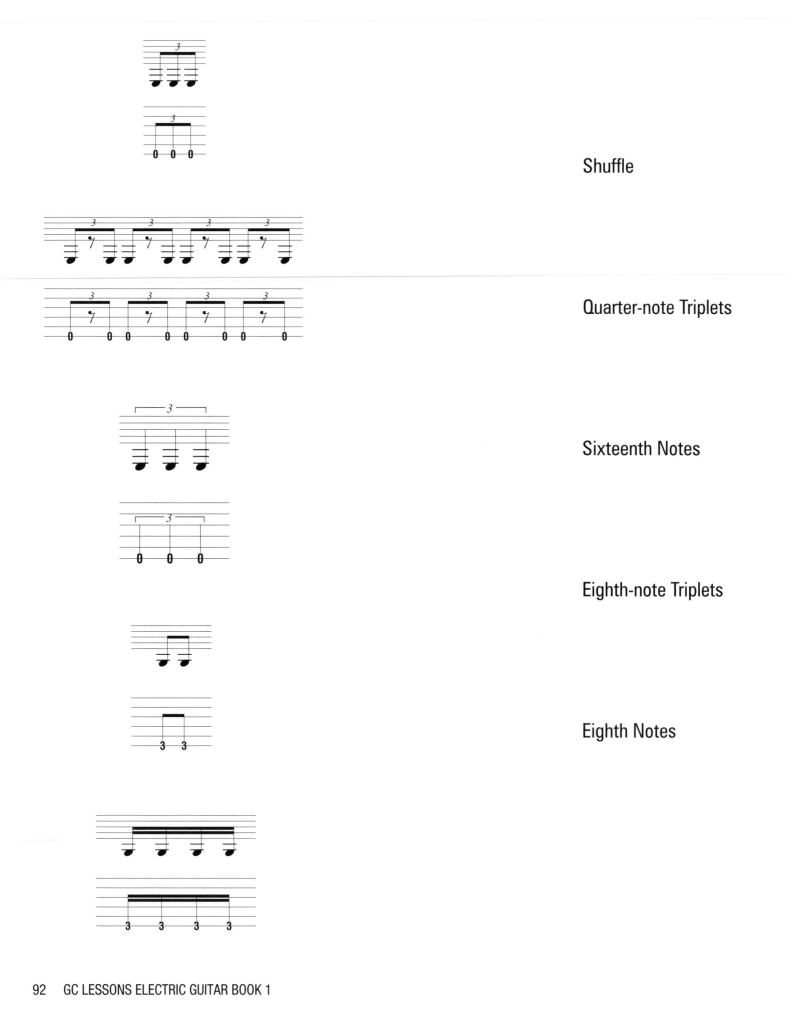

Shuffle

Quarter-note Triplets

Sixteenth Notes

Eighth-note Triplets

Eighth Notes

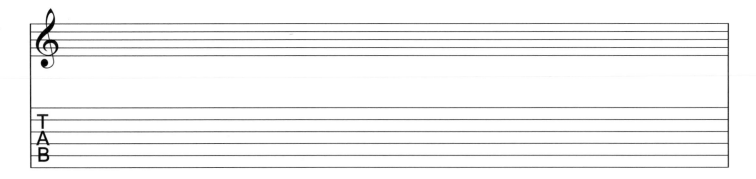

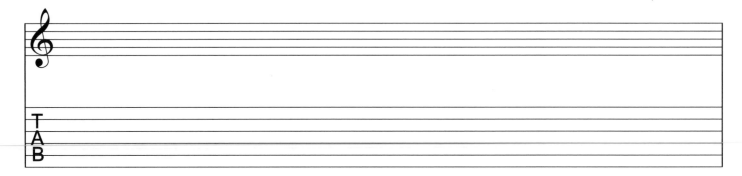

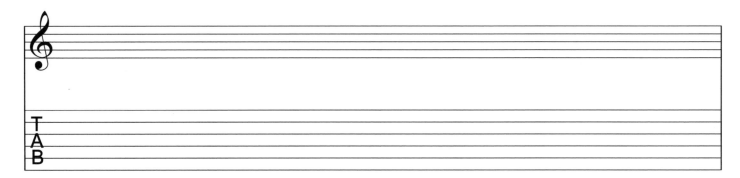